Inspirational Christmas Crafts

Inspirational Christmas Crafts

Madeline Hart

Sterling Publishing Co., Inc. New York
A Sterling/Chapelle Book

Chapelle Ltd.

Owner
Jo Packham

Editor
Karmen Quinney

Staff
Ann Bear, Kass Burchett, Rebecca Christensen, Marilyn Goff,
Shirley Heslop, Holly Hollingsworth, Shawn Hsu,
Susan Jorgensen, Pauline Locke, Ginger Mikkelsen,
Barbara Milburn, Linda Orton, Rhonda Rainey,
Leslie Ridenour, and Cindy Stoeckl

Designers
Joy Anckner, Marie Barber, Areta Bingham, Randa Black,
Holly Fuller, Sharon Ganske, Ann Hales, Kelly Henderson,
Mary Jo Hiney, and Judi Kauffman

Watercolors
Rhonda Rainey

Photographer
Kevin Dilley for Hazen Photography Studio

Photography Stylist
Leslie Liechty

Library of Congress Cataloging in Publication Data Available

A Sterling/Chapelle Book

10 9 8 7 6 5 4 3 2 1

First paperback edition published in 1999 by
Sterling Publishing Company, Inc.
387 Park Avenue South, New York, N.Y. 10016
Produced by Chapelle Ltd.
P.O. Box 9252, Newgate Station, Ogden, Utah 84409
© 1998 by Chapelle Ltd.
Distributed in Canada by Sterling Publishing
℅ Canadian Manda Group, One Atlantic Avenue, Suite 105
Toronto, Ontario, Canada M6K 3E7
Distributed in Great Britain and Europe by Cassell PLC
Wellington House, 125 Strand, London WC2R 0BB, England
Distributed in Australia by Capricorn Link (Australia) Pty Ltd.
P.O. Box 6651, Baulkham Hills, Business Centre, NSW 2153, Australia
Printed in Hong Kong
All rights reserved

Sterling ISBN 0-8069-1303-7 Trade
              0-8069-2457-8 Paper

We would like to offer our sincere appreciation for the valuable support given in this ever changing industry of new ideas, concepts, designs, and products. Several projects shown in this publication were created with the outstanding and innovative products developed by ADHESIVE TECH-NOLOGIES, (800) 458-3486; ALEENE'S PAINTS (209) 291-4444; ANCHOR; BUCILLA, (717) 384-2525; DMC, (201) 589-0606; DARICE INC., (800) 321-1494; DECO ART; DELTA PAINTS, (800) 423-4135; KREINIK, (800) 624-1928; JESSE JAMES AND CO., (610) 453-7899; MILL HILL BEADS, (800) 356-9438; NEEDLE NECESSITIES; PLAID ENTERPRISES INC.; WICHELT, (608) 788-4600; and ZWEIGART, (908) 271-1949.

If you have any questions or comments or would like information on specialty products featured in this book, please contact: Chapelle Ltd., Inc., P.O. Box 9252 Ogden, UT 84409 (801) 621-2777 • FAX (801) 621-2788

Table of Contents

Before beginning thoroughly read the general instructions. Also, before using any tools or materials listed in this book, read and follow manufacturer's instructions. Please refer to other sources for detailed instructions on techniques not covered in this book. The colors used in this book are simply suggestions. Substitute any color(s) desired.

Angel House Construction

General Supplies & Tools

- Craft knife
- Dremel tool
- Drill and drill bit
- Glue: craft; industrial-strength; wood
- Graphite paper
- Hot glue gun and glue sticks
- Jigsaw
- Needles
- Paintbrushes: assorted
- Pencil
- Ruler
- Sandpaper
- Scissors: craft; fabric
- Sponge
- Stylus
- Table saw
- Tack cloth
- Toothpicks
- Wood filler

Woods

Two types of wood were used for the construction of the angel houses featured in this book. Birch plywood is used for the ¼"-thick wood and pine is used for the ½"-thick wood. Both types of wood are readily available, durable, and easy to use.

Balsa wood has been used for doors. Because it is an extremely lightweight wood, it can easily be cut with a sharp craft knife.

Cutting Woods

When cutting the woods into the appropriate shapes according to the angel house patterns, the dimensions given are width x height. A table saw is recommended for cutting these pieces because it can accommodate the large pieces of wood.

A jigsaw is used to cut out windows and doors. Drilling a pilot hole first will allow the jigsaw blade to get into the area.

Transferring Windows & Doors

The first step in transferring windows and doors is to determine exactly where they should be placed. Three ways in which to determine placement are:

1. Simply enlarge the patterns according to the percentages given. Once the enlargements have been made, windows and doors should be in the correct positions. Next, tape the pattern onto the wood and, using graphite paper and a stylus, trace around the windows and doors until they are accurately transferred to the wood.

2. Mathematically calculate the positions. Since all outside dimensions have been provided, along with all window and door dimensions, the calculations can be determined using a graphing calculator.

3. Use personal judgment by placing windows and doors as desired. The actual transferring should be done using graphite paper and a stylus.

Cutting Windows & Doors

Once windows and doors have been transferred to the wood, they are ready to be cut out. If the window (or door) is positioned inside the dimensions of the piece of wood and cannot be accessed by cutting from an outside edge, a drill and ¼" drill bit should be used to drill pilot holes in each corner of the windows (and door). This enables the crafter to get a jigsaw into the wood to make the necessary cuts.

Sanding Woods

A little sanding will always be necessary. It is recommended that a medium-grit sandpaper be used for sanding rough edges. Additional sanding might be necessary when wood filler is used.

Assembling Angel Houses

The basic components for each angel house have been named in the material's list for each angel house. Begin the assembly process by placing the fronts and backs parallel to each other. Using wood glue, glue one side (pitched piece in most cases) to each end of fronts and backs, aligning all outside edges. Do not glue pitched pieces "inside" fronts and backs, as this will not allow the roofs to fit properly on top of the angel houses. Make certain all sides are glued on the outside of the fronts and backs. Allow glue to dry after each step.

Once fronts, backs, and sides have been glued together, glue the assembled angel house to base. Align base according to the individual instructions.

Do not glue roof pieces together or glue them onto the house until instructed to do so. All of the angel houses require some access to the inside from the top to secure windows, doors and door frames, curtains, and embellishments and this cannot be done once the roofs have been glued into position.

The angle of each roof is 45°, the dimensions of the roof pieces will vary only by the width of the wood being used. The smaller of the two pieces of wood should butt up against the outside long edge of the larger piece, thus making the appropriate 45° angle.

Installing Hardware

When hinge assemblies are necessary for hanging doors, it may seem impossible to work with such small pieces of hardware. A dremel tool is a small power tool that is perfect for these types of applications. Because the drill bits on a dremel are so small, they aid in providing pilot holes for the screws to install the appropriate hardware.

Painting Techniques
Base Coating

Base coating is used to do most of the painting on the angel houses. It is the application of acrylic paint to all painting surfaces for full, opaque coverage. The painting surfaces should be covered with two to three smooth, even coats of paint. It is better to apply several thin coats of paint rather than one heavy coat. Allow paint to dry between coats. If the paint causes the wood grain to raise, lightly sand the rough surfaces before applying additional coats of paint.

Washing

This technique refers to the application of acrylic paint to a surface for transparent coverage. It is done by mixing the paint with water in a 1:3 ratio (25% paint to 75% water). Thinned paint should never be applied to unsealed wood. Apply several coats to produce a soft, but deep, transparent color.

Decorating Inside of Houses

Once the angel house has been assembled, but before the roof has been glued into position, the inside of the angel house can be decorated. Be careful not to get too extravagant, because in most cases very little of the inside will actually show. However, every angel house should have those special touches that transform it from a house into a home. The inside walls can be painted or wallpapered with wallpaper or fabric that has adhesive on one side. Paint, carpet, wallpaper, fabric, and/or small tiles can be placed on the floor. If pictures are hung on the walls or furniture is added inside, they must be glued in place to prevent shifting once the angel house has been completed.

Adding Lights on the Inside
Small strands of electrical lights can be added so each angel house can be illuminated when desired. Lights can simply be added around the perimeter of the roof and/or windows similar to hanging Christmas lights around a house. If it is desired to have lights on the inside of the angel house for illumination, a notch must be cut in the base to accommodate the electrical cords.

Christmas Cottage on page 60.

Bible Cover Assembling

Note: To determine amount of cardboard needed for any size bible, measure width and height of front cover. Multiply width by four for total amount needed. For example: bible cover is 5" wide x 8" high. Multiply 5 x 4 for total cardboard amount of 20" x 8".

1. Measure width of bible front from edge of cover to where cover breaks and add ⅛" to width measurement. Add ¼" to height measurement. Cut four cardboard pieces according to measurements. Label one cardboard each as front, back, inner pocket front, and inner pocket back.

2. Cut designated fabric into two pieces that are ¾" larger all around than inner pocket front and inner pocket back.

3. Cut designated fabric into one piece that is 1-2" larger all around than front.

4. Cut designated fabric into one piece that is ¾" larger all around than back.

5. Measure width of spine from where cover breaks, front to back. Measure height of spine. Add 1½" to width measurement.

Double height measurement and add ¾". Cut one piece of designated fabric for spine according to measurements. Make a notation of the spine measurement for use in Step 8.

6. Place corresponding fabric cuts with cardboard pieces.

7. Embellish front and back as specified in each individual bible cover instructions.

8. Refer to General Instructions for Laminating on page 10. With wrong side down and flush to bottom, laminate ¾" of raw edge of spine fabric to one long edge of inner pocket front cardboard. Measure and mark spine width measurement from Step 5 onto wrong side of spine fabric from edge of cardboard. Laminate one long edge of inner pocket back cardboard onto spine fabric at mark, aligning top and bottom cardboard edges as shown.

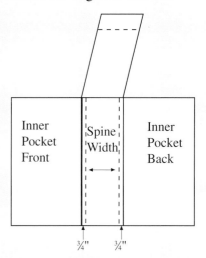

9. Place spine/cardboard piece on work surface with fabric wrong side up. Laminate extended spine fabric over onto itself, wrong sides together. Thoroughly flatten fabric.

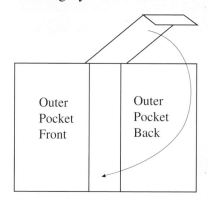

10. Turn spine/cardboard piece over. Laminate remaining ¾" of spine fabric up onto itself for a clean finish. Label this side as inside.

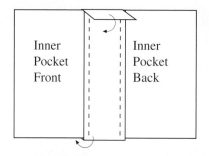

11. Laminate back cardboard with designated fabric.

12. Refer to General Instructions for Padding & Wrapping on page 11. Pad front cardboard with quilt batting. Trim quilt batting flush to edge.

13. Snugly wrap embellished front fabric around cardboard. Trim bulk from corners.

14. Fold back and press ¾" along one long side of inner pocket fabric pieces. Position one inner pocket fabric piece over inner pocket front inside, placing piece ½" from cardboard edge with spine. Wrap and glue raw edge of fabric around to outside of spine/cardboard piece. Trim bulk from corners. Repeat for second inner pocket.

15. Glue trim to underside edges of front or back as specified in each individual bible cover instructions.

16. With wrong sides together, glue front to inner pocket front. With wrong sides together, glue back to inner pocket back. Slip bible covers into inner pockets.

Embroidered Bible Cover on page 109.

Copper Leaf Application

1. Apply gold leaf adhesive using an old paintbrush. Tear copper leaf into small pieces and apply with an old paintbrush.

2. Set aside for one hour, then spray copper leafing with patina aging solution. Allow to set until copper leafing turns yellow and green.

Joint Compound Application

1. Attach desired item to board using tacky glue. Using spatula and fingertips, apply joint compound to all of board and part of item.

2. Attach tips and coupler to decorating bag. Fill decorating bag half full with joint compound. Practice required designs specified in project instructions on foil until comfortable with process. Make designs on tiles.

Laminating

Prepare a wet rag and a dry rag for constant hand cleaning. Cover work surface with newspaper. Pour enough tacky glue into disposable plastic or tin dish to cover bottom of dish. Place cardboard onto paper bag. Place fabric wrong side up on work surface.

1. Roll glue onto paint rollers in dish. Completely cover roller's surface, then roll off extra glue in dish. Paint entire surface of cardboard with glue. Make certain to follow any instructions regarding which side should be laminated if the cardboard is scored.

2. Place glued cardboard on fabric by flipping cardboard over onto wrong side of fabric and pressing in place.

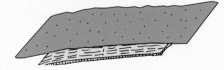

3. Flip fabric and cardboard over and smooth fabric completely. Eliminate any wrinkles immediately. Pay special attention to edges. Fabric should adhere to cardboard everywhere, especially at the edges.

4. Turn laminated cardboard over again. Trim out bulk from each corner. Use roller to paint edges of cardboard and fabric with glue.

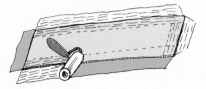

5. Wrap extended fabric over onto glued edges.

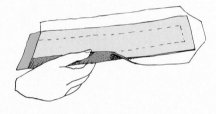

6. Double-check corners for fraying fabric, and dab frays with glue if necessary. Allow to dry for ten minutes.

Lace Bible Cover on page 108.

Padding & Wrapping

1. Lightly glue surface of cardboard shape. Place onto batting.

2. Trim batting flush to cardboard's edge, beveling scissors inward slightly.

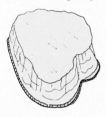

3. Place fabric wrong side up on work surface. Center padded cardboard over fabric.

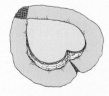

4. Glue 1" at inner edge of cardboard and wrap fabric onto glue. On opposite edge, glue and wrap another 1" worth of fabric onto cardboard. Pull fabric snugly. Continue to glue and wrap fabric onto cardboard a small amount at a time, pulling the fabric as snugly as possible. Exact shape of cardboard should not be altered when fabric is wrapped.

Resin Application

Casting resin is a clear polymer finish/liquid plastic. There are different types of resin on the market. Desired artwork should have all edges flat and be completely sealed with two to three coats of découpage medium or acrylic spray sealer before resin is applied.

Wood surfaces should be completely sealed with a base-coat of acrylic gesso before resin is applied. If wood surfaces are not sealed thoroughly, air bubbles will appear and may not burst.

1. Prepare working surface. Work in well ventilated area. Item(s) being coated with resin should be elevated from protected working surface area several inches so excess resin may drip off. *Note: Tray does not need to be elevated because resin will level out on tray surface.*

2. Measure ready-mix resin or one-to-one resin following manufacturer's instructions. Place into unwaxed plastic cup. Pour over entire surface as soon as mixed.

3. After pouring resin, air bubbles will rise and burst. Air bubbles are caused by resin de-gassing. Carbon dioxide is required for air bubbles to burst. Only exhale breathing on the surface or using a propane torch will cause air bubbles to burst.

On a small object, gentle exhale breathing on the surface will cause a few air bubbles to rise and disappear. A propane torch may be used for larger projects. Move torch side to side, 6" from surface. Manufacturer's suggest torching three times: (1) as soon as resin is poured, (2) ten minutes later, (3) fifteen minutes after second torching.

4. Use cardboard box to cover coated item to prevent dust from settling on surface during drying time. Drips may be sanded off after overnight drying using fine-grit sandpaper.

5. Clean-up resin by using acetone. Acrylic spray sealer may be used on project surface to help hide scratches if needed.

Ribbon Work

Bullion Lazy Daisy Stitch

1. Bring needle up at A. Keep ribbon flat, untwisted, and full. Go down through fabric at B and up at C, but do not pull through.

2. Loosely wrap ribbon around needle tip one to three times, as indicated in project stitch guide.

Holding finger over wrapped ribbon, pull needle through ribbon and fabric.

3. Completed Bullion Lazy Daisy Stitch.

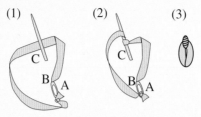

Couched Twisted Ribbon Stitch

1. Bring needle up at A. Extend ribbon its full length and twirl needle so ribbon coils, but not so tight it buckles.

2. Go down, piercing twisted ribbon at B. Pull needle through ribbon and fabric, allowing some of the ribbon to remain on the surface.

3. Make a short, tight Straight Stitch across ribbon base to couch twisted ribbon. Come up at C on one side of ribbon and go down at D on other side. This will cause ribbon to gather and pucker. The twisted ribbon base is tacked at varying intervals.

4. Completed Couched Twisted Ribbon Stitch.

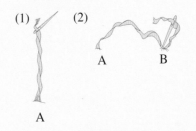

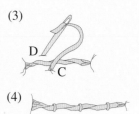

Couching Stitch

1. Complete a Straight Stitch base by coming up at A and going down at B (desired length of Straight Stitch). Make certain ribbon is flat and loose.

2. Make a short, tight Straight Stitch across ribbon base to couch Straight Stitch. Come up at C on one side of ribbon and go down at D on other side. The Straight Stitch base is tacked at varying intervals.

3. Completed Couching Stitch.

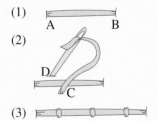

Cross-over Lazy Daisy

1. Bring needle up at A. Keep ribbon flat, untwisted, and full. Cross over to right, and go down through fabric at B and up at C. Pull ribbon to desired shape.

2. Go down at D making a Straight Stitch to tack loop.

3. Completed Cross-over Lazy Daisy.

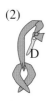

(1)   (2)   (3)

C A B D

Dahlia, Single Fold

1. Fold ends of ribbon forward diagonally. Press folds with iron for crisp edge. Pin folds in place.

2. Chain gather-stitch all petals together, stitching ¼" above raw edges. Tightly pull, gather, and secure thread. Join last petal to first. Trim raw edges ⅛" below stitches.

3. Completed Dahlia, Single Fold.

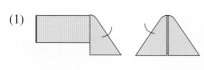

(1)

(2)

(3)

Daisy

1. Fold each length of ribbon forward to overlap at cut ends. Pin to hold.

2. Chain gather-stitch all petals together. Tightly pull, gather, and secure thread. Adjust gather so petals are evenly spaced. Follow project instructions for joining last petal to first petal.

3. Completed Daisy.

(1)

(2)

(3)

Fluting

1. Attach one ribbon end to fabric. Fold down diagonally and glue. Fold up and down diagonally again and glue. Repeat for entire area to be fluted. Fluting should extend ¼" past edge to be fluted.

Folded Leaf

1. Fold ends of ribbon forward diagonally.

2. Gather-stitch across bottom edge of folds. Tightly pull, gather, and secure thread.

3. Completed Folded Leaf.

(1)

(2)

Gathered Rose

(3)

1. Fold one short edge of ribbon forward diagonally.

2. Fold point back to ribbon keeping bottoms even.

3. Roll folded end of ribbon and secure with thread. Gather-stitch half of remaining ribbon. Pull thread and wrap gather around folded ribbon.

4. Gather-stitch remaining ribbon. Wrap gather around.

5. Completed Gathered Rose.

(1)

(2)

(3)

(4)

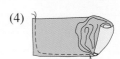

(5)

Knotted and Looped Ribbon Stitch

1. Bring ribbon to surface. Tie a knot in ribbon ¼" from entry

point, or the amount indicated in project instructions.

2. Fold ribbon over on itself and form knot. Stitch into ribbon and fabric directly next to base of entry point to complete stitch, allowing entire looped and knotted ribbon to remain above surface.

3. Completed Knotted and Looped Ribbon Stitch.

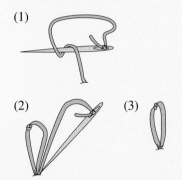

Looped Bow
1. Leaving a length of ribbon for one tail, make a figure eight with desired size loops. Hold ribbon in center with thumb and forefinger and make second figure eight on top of first.

2. Continue until desired number of loops are formed and leave a second tail. Pinch together center of loops.

3. Wrap and knot craft wire around center to secure for completed Looped Bow.

Looped Ribbon Stitch
1. Bring needle up at A. Form small loop and go down at B, piercing ribbon.

2. Completed Looped Ribbon Stitch.

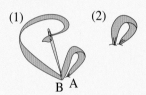

Outline Stitch
1. Bring needle up at end of line at A. Keep thread to the right and above needle. Push needle down at B and back up at C. Continue for completed Outline Stitch.

Overcast Stitch
1. Bring needle up at A, wrap thread over fabric edge at B. Bring needle back up at C. Continue for completed Overcast Stitch.

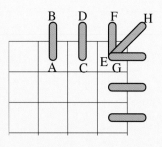

Pencil Flower
1. Cut ribbon into 12" length. Using two pencils held closely together, slip ribbon through center of pencils, with one ribbon end extended 3". Weave ribbon around pencils so each pencil has three loops of ribbon.

2. Take top end of ribbon and wrap it down, under, and up around the center of pencils two times while holding the ribbon loops together.

3. Take opposite end of ribbon and wrap it up, under, and up around center of the pencils while cinching ribbon loops tighter. Take ribbon ends and tie them into a double knot at center of one side. Ribbon ends must be at opposite ends of wrapped ribbon before tying into knots. Slip Pencil Flower off pencils.

4. Completed Pencil Flower.

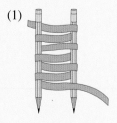

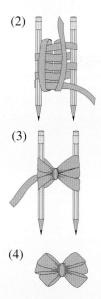

(2)

(3)

(4)

Petal Flower

1. Beginning ¼" from edge, trace specified half circles on ribbon at equal intervals. Butt circles up to each other. Trim fabric ¼" past last half circle. Gather-stitch on traced half circles with continuous gather stitch.

2. Tightly gather and secure thread. Join last petal to first and secure thread.

3. Completed Petal Flower.

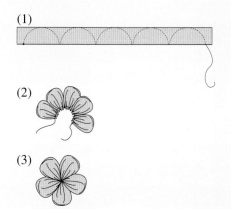

(1)

(2)

(3)

Ribbon Stitch

1. Come up through fabric at A. Lay ribbon flat on fabric. At end of the stitch, pierce ribbon with the needle at B. Slowly pull length of ribbon through to back, allow ends of ribbon to curl. If ribbon is pulled too tight, the effect can be lost. Vary petals and leaves by adjusting length, tension of ribbon before piercing, and how loosely or tightly ribbon is pulled down through itself.

2. Completed Ribbon Stitch.

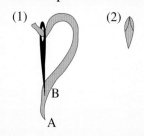

(1)   (2)

B

A

Ribbon Stitch, 1-Twist

1. Bring ribbon up through fabric at A. Twist ribbon one time. Go down at B, piercing ribbon. Slowly pull to back.

2. Completed 1-Twist Ribbon Stitch.

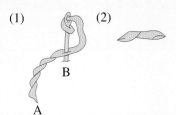

(1)   (2)

B

A

Rosette

1. Beginning at one end, fold end forward at right angle. Fold

vertical end of ribbon forward upon itself.

2. Fold horizontal end of ribbon back and at right angle. Fold vertical ribbon over once. Continue folding ribbon back and over forming the rosette.

3. Upon reaching center mark, secure with a stitch, leaving needle and thread attached. Gather-stitch bottom edge of remaining ribbon. Gather tightly. Wrap gathered ribbon around bud.

4. Completed Rosette.

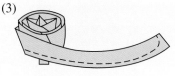

(1)

(2)

(3)

(4)

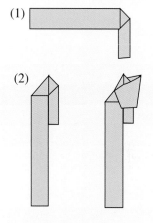

Star Petal

1. Fold ends of ribbon forward diagonally. Fold second fold halfway back on itself. Tack at base. Trim excess ribbon ⅛" past stitching.

2. Completed Star Petal.

(1)

(2)

Straight Stitch

1. This stitch may be taut or loose, depending on desired effect. Come up at A and go down at B at desired length.

2. Completed Straight Stitch.

(1)   (2)

A
x

B

Kissing Ball on page 25.

Stenciling with Paste

1. Mix decorating paste with specified paint color until desired color is achieved. Lay stencil over tile and hold in place with hand. Smooth decorating paste to ⅛" thickness over stencil using a butter knife. Carefully lift stencil off tile using both hands.

2. Dry stenciled design with a blow dryer on low heat. The heat will smooth out the medium. Wash and dry stencil, then repeat process on remaining tiles.

Texturizing Wood

1. Apply texture paste to right side of wood roof using a palette

knife. Apply in same manner as frosting a cake.

2. Scratch through paste in an up and down and side to side motion using a plastic fork to create a thatch-like appearance. Clean off fork regularly to prevent build-up of paste.

3. Repeat process on left side of wood roof and then on floor. Allow to dry overnight.

Sharing Christmas Traditions

Chapter One

Angel Wreath

Materials
- Copper leafing
- Floral moss: green
- Gold leaf adhesive
- Grapevine wreath: 27" dia.
- Papier-mâché angels (3)
- Patina aging solution: rust
- Pepper berries
- Pinecones: large (9)
- Sheer ribbon: 1½"-wide green/rust floral (2 yds.); 3"-wide gold (7 yds.)
- Silk pine garland (6')
- Silk poinsettias: large (6)
- Wire: 14 gauge; 20 gauge

General Supplies & Tools
- Fabric scissors
- Glue gun and glue sticks
- Needlenose pliers
- Paintbrushes: old
- Wire cutters

Instructions
1. Wrap pine garland around wreath five to six times. Secure to wreath using 14 gauge wire and needlenose pliers. Arrange garland as desired.

2. Refer to General Instructions for Copper Leaf Application on page 9. Apply copper leaf to pinecones.

3. Arrange pinecones on wreath and hot-glue in place. Hot-glue miniature pinecones, pepper berries, and moss to wreath to fill in open spaces. Hot-glue poinsettias to wreath.

4. Refer to General Instructions for Looped Bow on page 14. Without cutting gold ribbon, make a large 3-loop bow. Secure base of bow with 20 gauge wire and hot-glue to wreath. Gently wrap and twist ribbon around wreath and make another bow. Hot-glue bow in place. Repeat process around entire wreath. Make some bows 4-loop and make last bow at bottom of wreath 6-loop.

5. Cut floral sheer ribbon into four equal lengths. Make each ribbon into a 3-loop bow. Glue bows to wreath as desired.

6. Attach angels to bottom of wreath using 20 gauge wire.

7. Form a loop for hanging using 20 gauge wire and needlenose pliers. Attach to center top of wreath.

Cherub Frame

Photo on page 20.

Materials
- Acrylic paint: gold
- Assorted rhinestones: small
- Frame: 5" x 7" flat-surfaced
- Gift tag

General Supplies & Tools
- Craft scissors
- Découpage medium
- Industrial-strength glue
- Paintbrush

Instructions
1. Paint frame gold.

2. Cut out motif from gift tag.

3. Refer to photo. Découpage motif to top of frame following manufacturer's instructions. Allow to dry.

4. Randomly glue rhinestones onto motif and frame. *Note: Place a favorite quotation, verse, or picture into frame.*

Chair Cover

Photo on page 22.

Materials
- Coordinating bias tape: (2 yds.)
- Lining: (4½ yds.)
- Two contrasting fabrics: 52"-wide (1½ yds. each for standard-size chair)

General Supplies & Tools
- Coordinating thread
- Fabric scissors
- Sewing machine
- Straight pins

Piece #1 (A + 2") x (B + 2")
  Cut 1
Piece #2 (C + 2") x (D + 2")
  Cut 1
Piece #3 (E + 2") x (F + 2")
  Cut 2—1 + lining
Piece #4 (G + 2") x (H + 2")
  Cut 4—2 + linings
Piece #5 (I + 2") x 8"
  Cut 8—4 + linings
  (contrast)
Piece #6 (J + 6") x 45"
  Cut 1
Piece #7 8" x 55"
  Cut 4—2 + 2 contrast

Instructions
The amount of fabric needed will vary according to chair size. Adjust as needed. Refer to Diagram 1 as needed.

1. Working wrong side out, place piece #1 in position on chair. Fold and pin to form square corners. Stitch.

2. Return to chair and pin piece #1 to piece #2 where chair back meets chair seat. Stitch, allowing a generous seam allowance.

3. Attach 2 yd. piece of bias tape to edge of seam allowance, leaving 2" on each side free. This makes hidden ties to hold seat firmly in place.

4. Prepare chair back piece #6 by pressing self lining into place and stitching. Return to chair and pin piece #6 into place. Form pleats as desired, keeping bottom even with floor. Stitch. Tack "tuck" up while stitching.

5. Prepare skirt by stitching together pieces 5-4-5-3-5-4-5. Repeat with lining pieces. Stitch lining to skirt at bottom. Turn and press. Baste across top. Pin into place on three sides of chair seat, adjusting bottom to floor and front pleats into place. Stitch, catching only one side of back pleats.

6. Stitch uncaught sides of back pleats to cover back, starting at bottom and stitching over existing seams.

7. Turn cover right side out and adjust on chair. Pin back of rear pleat into place. Pin front of back pleat under tacked up raw edge. Top-stitch back pleats into place starting on one side of chair cover across front of "tuck" to other side, catching turned up raw edges in the process.

8. Prepare back sash by placing wrong sides together. Stitch around three sides. Turn and press. Determine best placement for sash, then stitch into place, folding raw edges under. Tie sash and hidden ties into bows.

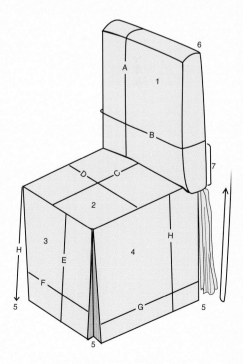

Diagram 1

Advent Drawers

Photo on page 24.

Materials

- Acrylic gesso
- Acrylic paints: coordinating colors
- Acrylic sealer: matte
- Birch plywood: ¼"-thick (½ sheet); ⅛"-thick (8')
- Dollhouse stair balusters: 3" (24)
- Miniature drawer pulls (24)
- Papers: assorted decorative napkins; wrapping paper; greeting cards; metallic gold wrapping (1 sheet); numerals in assorted fonts
- Verdigris finish

General Supplies & Tools

- Craft scissors: small, sharp
- Découpage medium: antique
- Drill and drill bit
- Embossing tool
- Jigsaw
- Paintbrushes
- Wood glue
- Wood putty

Instructions

1. Cut ¼" plywood into seven 14¼" x 4¾" pieces for shelves and six 13½" x ½" pieces for drawer stoppers using a jigsaw. Cut ⅛" plywood into twenty-four 3¼" x 2½" pieces for drawer backs, twenty-four 3¼" x 3" pieces for drawer fronts, twenty-four 3⅛" x 4½" pieces for drawer bottoms, and forty-eight 4½" x 2½" pieces for drawer sides.

2. Refer to Diagram 1 and drill two holes in both ends of each shelf, 1" in from each side. Glue a baluster rail in each hole of one shelf. Secure next shelf on top of rails with glue. Continue process until all shelves are stacked. Fill holes with wood putty.

Diagram 1

3. Refer to Diagram 2 and glue drawer stoppers to back edge of shelves.

Diagram 2

4. Refer to Diagram 3 and assemble drawers. Glue sides to bottom, then glue fronts and backs to bottom.

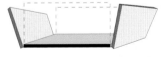

Diagram 3

5. Apply a coat of acrylic gesso onto shelf unit and drawers, then paint using desired coordinating paint color.

6. Cut 3¼" x 3" squares and individual motifs from assorted papers for 18 of the drawer fronts. Cut metallic wrapping paper into 3¼" x 3" squares for remaining drawer fronts. Cut out numerals.

7. Emboss opposite side of metallic wrapping paper using an embossing tool and desired design. Paint verdigris finish onto front side of paper following manufacturer's instructions.

8. Découpage paper squares to drawer fronts. Allow to dry.

9. Paint drawers for motifs using two-three coordinating colors. Allow to dry, then découpage motifs to drawer fronts.

10. Apply a second coat of découpage to all drawer fronts. Allow to dry.

11. Lightly paint numerals using a coordinating paint color. Allow to dry. Découpage numerals to drawer fronts. Allow to dry.

12. Spray advent drawers with matte acrylic sealer.

13. Randomly attach drawer pulls to drawer fronts.

Kissing Ball

Photo on page 25.

Materials
- Ball: 5"-dia. purchased gold-leafed papier-mâché
- Floral picks: purple/pink berry; gold cedar; silk fern; 3" flocked leaf; miniature gold pinecone; large ivory stamen (7 bunches); small gold stamen (4 bunches)
- Ribbons: silk — 13mm gold (1⅝ yds.); organza — 1"-wide gold (1 yd.); wire-edge —1½"-wide burgundy/gold (1 yd.); 1½"-wide red/gold wire-edge (1⅛ yds.)

General Supplies & Tools
- Coordinating thread
- Fabric scissors
- Glue gun and glue sticks
- Hand-sewing needles

Instructions
Refer to General Instructions on pages 12-16 for ribbon work that is used for this project.

1. Snip leaves from silk fern floral pick. Refer to photo for placement and hot-glue leaves around top of ball. Snip leaves from cedar floral pick and hot-glue leaves around top of ball, slightly lower than fern leaves.

2. Cut burgundy/gold wire-edge ribbon into four 8" lengths and sew each ribbon into a Petal Flower. Hot-glue a bunch of gold stamen into center of each petal flower. Hot-glue two or three flocked fern leaves to back of petal flowers. Hot-glue petal flowers to ball.

3. Cut red/gold wire-edge ribbon into four 10" lengths and sew each ribbon into a Gathered Rose. Hot-glue two or three flocked fern leaves to back of gathered roses. Hot-glue gathered roses to ball.

4. Snip leaves, pinecones, and groups of berries from floral picks and hot-glue leaves, pinecones, and berries to ball.

5. Hot-glue ivory stamen bunches to ball.

6. Cut silk ribbon into eight 7" lengths and make each ribbon into a Pencil Flower. Hot-glue pencil flowers to ball.

7. Hot-glue additional fern leaves around top of ball.

8. Tie organza ribbon into a Looped Bow. Hot-glue bow to top of ball.

Scriptural Frame

Materials
- Acrylic paint: metallic gold
- Paper: 8½" x 11" handmade white with gold; 15" x 20" wrapping
- Picture frame: 9" x 11" wood

General Supplies & Tools
- Craft knife
- Craft scissors
- Découpage medium
- Old paintbrushes

Instructions
1. Paint entire frame metallic gold.

2. Découpage front, sides, and inside opening edge of frame. Smooth wrapping paper onto glued areas of frame. Trim excess paper from edges using a craft knife. Paint an even layer of glue over paper to seal.

3. Photocopy desired bible verse on specialty paper at a copy center, reducing or enlarging as necessary to fit frame opening. Trim paper to fit inside frame, then assemble in frame.

Festive Serving Tray

Materials
- Acrylic paints: green, dk. green, dk. red
- Crackle medium
- Decorating paste
- Grout: white
- Liquid resin
- Spray paint: golden oak
- Stencil: 4" rose
- Tiles: 4¼" square white, matte-finish (12)
- Wood tray: 20" x 15"

General Supplies & Tools
- Blow dryer
- Butter knife
- Craft glue
- Mixing bowl
- Paintbrushes

Instructions
1. Paint tray dk. green. Allow to dry. Apply crackle medium following manufacturer's instructions, then paint tray in a lighter shade of green. Allow to dry.

2. Cover back of tiles with craft glue and glue to inside of tray.

3. Prepare, apply, and clean tile grout around tiles in tray following manufacturer's instructions.

4. Mix decorating paste with dk. red paint until desired color is achieved. Refer to General Instructions for Stenciling with Paste on page 16. Stencil roses on tiles.

5. Paint grout between tiles dk. green. Apply a light coat of spray paint on tiles.

6. Refer to General Instructions for Resin Application on pages 11-12. Apply two coats resin to tiles inside tray.

Finial Frame

Photo on page 30.

Materials
- Acrylic paint: gold, ivory, antique white
- Acrylic sealer: matte
- Antiquing medium: brown
- Finials: 6½" curtain (2)
- Glass: 5" x 7" (2)
- Photograph: as desired
- Plywood: 3" x 7" x ½"
- Wrapping paper or greeting cards

General Supplies & Tools
- Craft knife
- Craft scissors: small, sharp
- Glue gun and glue sticks
- Paintbrushes
- Reverse découpage medium
- Router
- Sponge

Instructions
1. Cut out desired wrapping paper or greeting cards using craft scissors. Place and arrange designs around an oval shape on back of one piece of glass, overlapping as necessary.

2. Attach designs to back of one piece of glass using reverse découpage medium and following manufacturer's instructions. Paint areas not covered by designs using gold paint and a sponge. Allow to dry, then sponge-paint over gold using antique white paint. Trim excess paper from edges of glass using a craft knife.

3. Make a ¼" groove down center of 7" length of plywood base using a router.

4. Paint base and finials ivory. Apply brown antiquing medium to base and finials following manufacturer's instructions. Allow to dry, then dry-brush gold.

5. Spray base and finials with matte acrylic sealer.

6. Refer to photo for placement and hot-glue finials to base. Sandwich photograph between glass pieces. Place glass in base.

Holiday Plates

Photo on page 31.

Materials
- Enamel extender
- Enamel glaze: clear satin
- Enamel paints: gold, silver, white
- Glass plates (3)
- Nail polish remover: non-acetone

General Supplies & Tools
- Artist's blending stomp: small
- Liquid dish soap
- Paintbrushes
- Paper towels
- Waxed paper

Instructions

1. Wash plates using liquid dish soap. Dry plates.

2. Cover work surface with waxed paper. Place plates face down on waxed paper. Add a few drops of enamel extender to paints. Paint entire back of one plate using even, vertical strokes.

3. Dip blending stomp into nail polish remover and "draw" desired design on back of plate, beginning at center of plate and working out toward edges. Work quickly before paint dries and wipe excess paint from blending stomp using a paper towel, then re-dip blending stomp in nail polish remover. Repeat process using remaining plates and paints.

4. Apply a coat of enamel glaze to back of plate for durability. *Note: Always hand-wash plates.*

Découpage Plate

Materials
- Acrylic paint: metallic gold
- Acrylic sealer: clear
- Card: desired Christmas
- Glass plate: 15"
- Gold leafing
- Gold leafing adhesive
- Tissue paper: Christmas print (1 sheet)

General Supplies & Tools
- Craft knife
- Craft scissors
- Liquid dish soap
- Old paintbrush
- Reverse découpage medium
- Sponge

Instructions

1. Wash plate using liquid dish soap. Dry plate.

2. Tear tissue paper into 1" pieces.

3. Paint gold leaf adhesive on underside of plate. Allow to dry. Apply gold leafing to adhesive, leaving blotchy for a mottled appearance.

4. Cut card to fit center of plate using craft scissors. Paint reverse découpage medium on bottom center of plate. Position card right side down over glue and press from center out to remove any air bubbles.

5. Apply torn tissue papers right side down to underside of plate using reverse découpage medium in same manner as with card and overlapping as necessary to cover entire back of plate.

6. Paint underside of plate using reverse découpage medium. Allow to dry. If necessary, trim any excess paper and leafing from edge of plate using a craft knife.

7. Paint underside of plate with two coats of metallic gold acrylic paint.

8. Spray back of plate with clear acrylic sealer. *Note: Carefully clean plate with a damp sponge. Do not immerse plate in water.*

28 over two threads, the finished design size is 7⅞" x 12⅛". The fabric was cut 14" x 19".

Stitch Count 110 x 170

Other Fabrics	Design Size
Aida 11	10" x 15½"
Aida 18	6⅛" x 9½"
Hardanger 22	5" x 7¾"
Linen 32 over 2	6⅞" x 10⅝"

Anchor　　**DMC**

Step 1: Cross Stitch (2 strands)

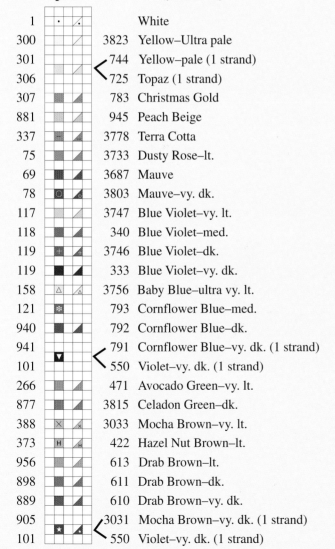

Anchor	DMC	
1		White
300	3823	Yellow–Ultra pale
301	744	Yellow–pale (1 strand)
306	725	Topaz (1 strand)
307	783	Christmas Gold
881	945	Peach Beige
337	3778	Terra Cotta
75	3733	Dusty Rose–lt.
69	3687	Mauve
78	3803	Mauve–vy. dk.
117	3747	Blue Violet–vy. lt.
118	340	Blue Violet–med.
119	3746	Blue Violet–dk.
119	333	Blue Violet–vy. dk.
158	3756	Baby Blue–ultra vy. lt.
121	793	Cornflower Blue–med.
940	792	Cornflower Blue–dk.
941	791	Cornflower Blue–vy. dk. (1 strand)
101	550	Violet–vy. dk. (1 strand)
266	471	Avocado Green–vy. lt.
877	3815	Celadon Green–dk.
388	3033	Mocha Brown–vy. lt.
373	422	Hazel Nut Brown–lt.
956	613	Drab Brown–lt.
898	611	Drab Brown–dk.
889	610	Drab Brown–vy. dk.
905	3031	Mocha Brown–vy. dk. (1 strand)
101	550	Violet–vy. dk. (1 strand)

Step 2: Backstitch (1 strand)

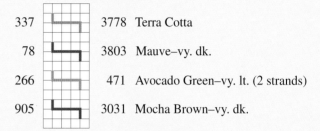

	DMC	
337	3778	Terra Cotta
78	3803	Mauve–vy. dk.
266	471	Avocado Green–vy. lt. (2 strands)
905	3031	Mocha Brown–vy. dk.

Step 3: French Knot (1 strand)

	DMC	
306	725	Topaz
905	3031	Mocha Brown–vy. dk.

Step 4: Long Stitch (1 strand)

	DMC	
300	3823	Yellow–Ultra pale
306	725	Topaz (2 strands)
307	783	Christmas Gold (2 strands)

Top Right

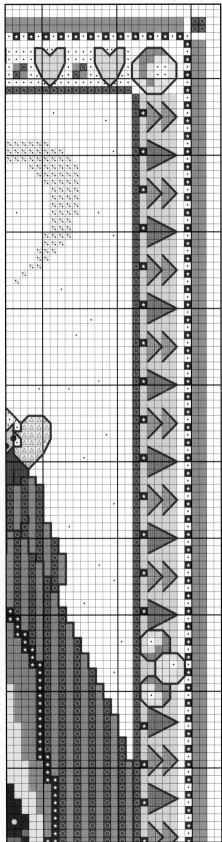

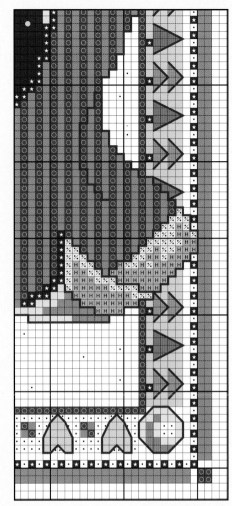

Bottom Right

*Let your light so shine before
men, that they may see your
good works, and glorify your
Father which is in heaven.*
St. Matthew 5:16

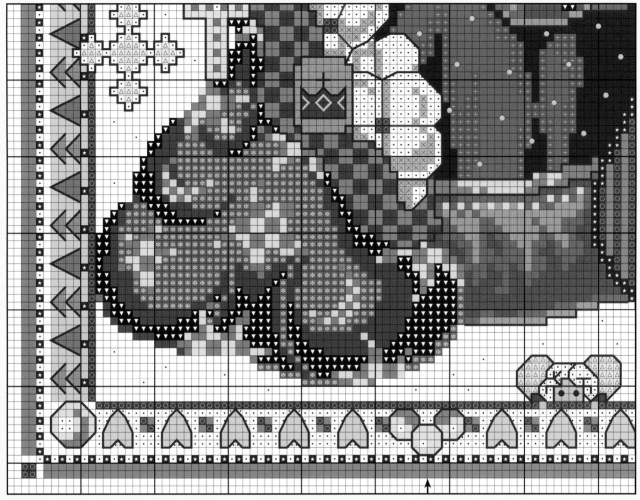

Bottom Left

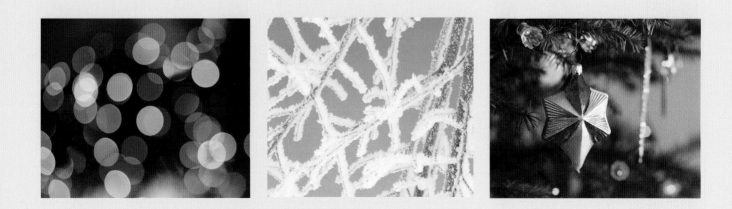

Christmas Fruit

Stitching Information
Stitched on Cream/Gold Lugana

25 over two threads, the finished design size is 14¼" x 7⅞". The fabric was cut 20" x 14".

Stitch count 178 x 98

Other Fabrics	Design Size
Aida 11	16⅛" x 8⅞"
Aida 14	12¾" x 7"
Aida 18	9⅞" x 5⅛"
Hardanger 22	8⅛" x 4½"
Linen 32 over 2	11⅛" x 6⅛"

Anchor **DMC**

Step 1: Cross Stitch (2 strands)

Anchor		DMC	
926	·		Ecru
4146		950	Peach Pecan–dk.
868	–	758	Terra Cotta–lt.
868		758	Terra Cotta–lt. (1 strand)
337	◎	3778	Terra Cotta (1 strand)
337		3778	Terra Cotta (1 strand)
894		223	Shell Pink–med. (1 strand)
893		224	Shell Pink–lt.
894	✿	223	Shell Pink–med.
896	⊞	3722	Shell Pink
896		3722	Shell Pink (1 strand)
970		315	Antique Mauve–vy. dk. (1 strand)
897		221	Shell Pink–vy. dk. (1 strand)
872		3740	Antique Violet–dk. (1 strand)
969		316	Antique Mauve–med.
104		210	Lavender–med. (1 strand)
870		3042	Antique Violet–lt. (1 strand)
110		208	Lavender–vy. dk. (1 strand)
872		3740	Antique Violet–dk. (1 strand)
869	▽	3743	Antique Violet–vy. lt.
871		3041	Antique Violet–med. (1 strand)
118		340	Blue Violet–med. (1 strand)
842		3013	Khaki Green–lt.
844		3012	Khaki Green–med.
844	⁙	3012	Khaki Green–med. (1 strand)
373		3045	Yellow Beige–dk. (1 strand)
845	✦	3011	Khaki Green–dk.
845	★	3011	Khaki Green–dk.
845		3011	Khaki Green–med. (1 strand)
889		370	Mustard–med. (1 strand)
845		3011	Khaki Green–med. (1 strand)
872	✕	3740	Antique Violet–med. (1 strand)
846		3051	Green Gray–dk.
387	٪	822	Beige Gray–Lt.
373		422	Hazel Nut Brown–lt.
887		372	Mustard–lt. (1 strand)
887		3046	Yellow Beige–med. (1 strand)
886	☐	3047	Yellow Beige–lt.

Top Center

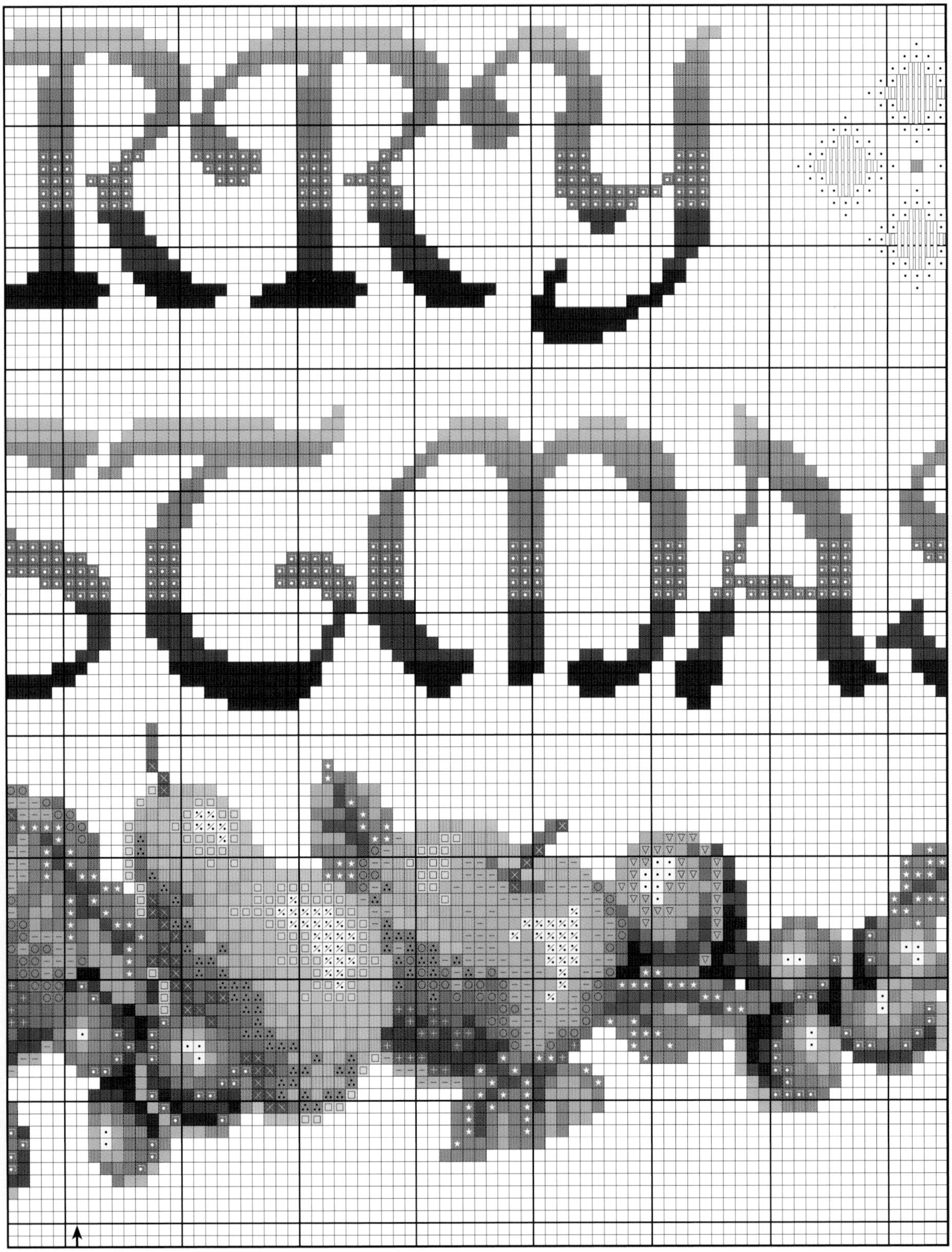

Top Right   Optional Phrase   Top Left

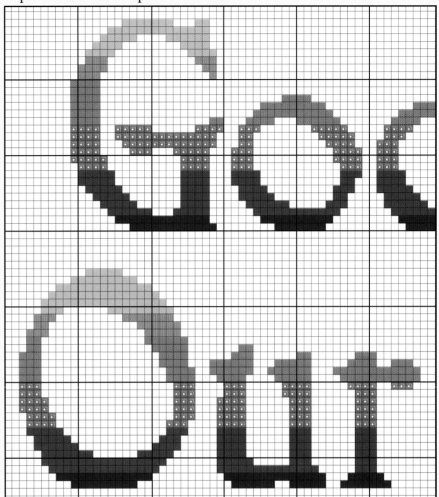

And when they were come into the house, they saw the young child with Mary his mother, and fell down, and worshiped him: and they had opened their treasure, they presented unto him gifts: gold, and frankincense, and myrrh.

St. Matthew 2:11

Christmas Angel

Photo on page 45.
Stitching Information
Stitched on Quaker cloth 28

over two threads, the finished design size is 14" x 15⅛". The fabric was cut 20" x 22". See Chart Diagram on page 47 for graph page placement.

Stitch Count 196 x 212

Other Fabrics	Design Size
Aida 11	17⅞" x 19¼"
Aida 18	10⅞" x 11¾"
Hardanger 22	8⅞" x 9⅝"
Linen 32 over 2	12¼" x 13¼"

Anchor **DMC**

Step 1: Cross Stitch (2 strands)

Anchor		DMC	Color
1			White
926			Ecru
300		745	Yellow–lt. pale
306		725	Topaz
891		676	Old Gold–lt.
373		3045	Yellow Beige–dk.
366		951	Peach Pecan–lt.
881		945	Peach Beige
868		758	Terra Cotta–lt.
337		3778	Terra Cotta
1014		3830	Terra Cotta–dk.
49		963	Wild Rose–vy. lt.
25		3326	Rose–lt.
11		3328	Salmon–dk.
894		223	Shell Pink–med.
896		3721	Shell Pink–dk.
20		498	Christmas Red–dk.
70		3685	Mauve–dk.
72		902	Garnet–vy. dk.
108		211	Lavender–lt.
95		554	Violet–lt.
118		340	Blue Violet–med.
167		597	Turquoise
1039		3809	Turquoise–vy. dk.
149		311	Navy Blue–med.
264		472	Avocado Green–ultra lt.

Anchor		DMC	Color
266		3347	Yellow Green–med.
268		937	Avocado Green–med.
862		935	Avocado Green–dk.
879		500	Blue Green–vy. dk.
899		3782	Mocha Brown–lt.
392		3032	Mocha Brown–med.
905		3781	Mocha Brown–dk.
381		3031	Mocha Brown–vy. dk.
898		611	Drab Brown–dk.
830		644	Beige Gray–med.
903		640	Beige Gray–vy. dk.
1			White (1 strand)
899		3782	Mocha Brown–lt. (1 strand)
926			Ecru (1 strand)
891		676	Old Gold–lt. (1 strand)
300		745	Yellow–lt. pale (1 strand)
306		725	Topaz (1 strand)
306		725	Topaz (1 strand)
307		783	Christmas Gold (1 strand)
307		783	Christmas Gold (1 strand)
309		781	Topaz–dk. (1 strand)
891		676	Old Gold–lt. (1 strand)
373		3045	Yellow Beige–dk. (1 strand)
891		676	Old Gold–lt. (1 strand)
323		722	Orange Spice–lt. (1 strand)

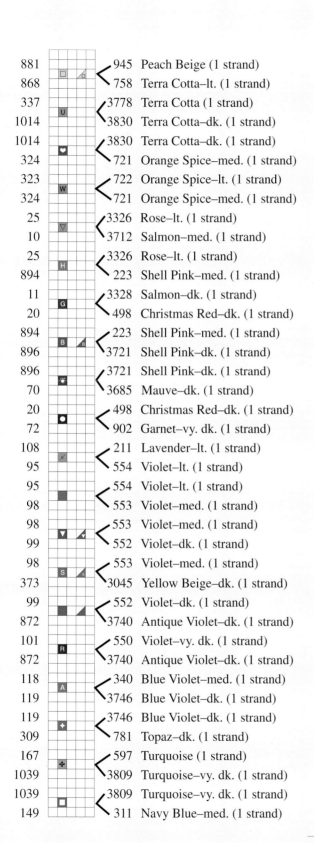

881	945	Peach Beige (1 strand)
868	758	Terra Cotta–lt. (1 strand)
337	3778	Terra Cotta (1 strand)
1014	3830	Terra Cotta–dk. (1 strand)
1014	3830	Terra Cotta–dk. (1 strand)
324	721	Orange Spice–med. (1 strand)
323	722	Orange Spice–lt. (1 strand)
324	721	Orange Spice–med. (1 strand)
25	3326	Rose–lt. (1 strand)
10	3712	Salmon–med. (1 strand)
25	3326	Rose–lt. (1 strand)
894	223	Shell Pink–med. (1 strand)
11	3328	Salmon–dk. (1 strand)
20	498	Christmas Red–dk. (1 strand)
894	223	Shell Pink–med. (1 strand)
896	3721	Shell Pink–dk. (1 strand)
896	3721	Shell Pink–dk. (1 strand)
70	3685	Mauve–dk. (1 strand)
20	498	Christmas Red–dk. (1 strand)
72	902	Garnet–vy. dk. (1 strand)
108	211	Lavender–lt. (1 strand)
95	554	Violet–lt. (1 strand)
95	554	Violet–lt. (1 strand)
98	553	Violet–med. (1 strand)
98	553	Violet–med. (1 strand)
99	552	Violet–dk. (1 strand)
98	553	Violet–med. (1 strand)
373	3045	Yellow Beige–dk. (1 strand)
99	552	Violet–dk. (1 strand)
872	3740	Antique Violet–dk. (1 strand)
101	550	Violet–vy. dk. (1 strand)
872	3740	Antique Violet–dk. (1 strand)
118	340	Blue Violet–med. (1 strand)
119	3746	Blue Violet–dk. (1 strand)
119	3746	Blue Violet–dk. (1 strand)
309	781	Topaz–dk. (1 strand)
167	597	Turquoise (1 strand)
1039	3809	Turquoise–vy. dk. (1 strand)
1039	3809	Turquoise–vy. dk. (1 strand)
149	311	Navy Blue–med. (1 strand)

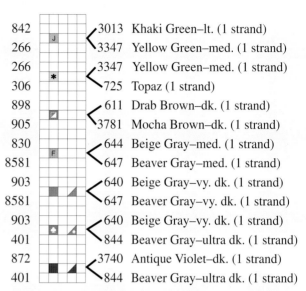

842	3013	Khaki Green–lt. (1 strand)
266	3347	Yellow Green–med. (1 strand)
266	3347	Yellow Green–med. (1 strand)
306	725	Topaz (1 strand)
898	611	Drab Brown–dk. (1 strand)
905	3781	Mocha Brown–dk. (1 strand)
830	644	Beige Gray–med. (1 strand)
8581	647	Beaver Gray–med. (1 strand)
903	640	Beige Gray–vy. dk. (1 strand)
8581	647	Beaver Gray–vy. dk. (1 strand)
903	640	Beige Gray–vy. dk. (1 strand)
401	844	Beaver Gray–ultra dk. (1 strand)
872	3740	Antique Violet–dk. (1 strand)
401	844	Beaver Gray–ultra dk. (1 strand)

Step 2: Backstitch (1 strand)

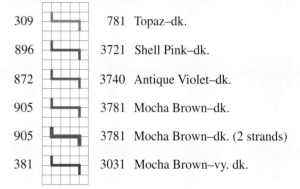

309	781	Topaz–dk.
896	3721	Shell Pink–dk.
872	3740	Antique Violet–dk.
905	3781	Mocha Brown–dk.
905	3781	Mocha Brown–dk. (2 strands)
381	3031	Mocha Brown–vy. dk.

Step 3: Long Stitch (1 strand)

| 1014 | 3830 | Terra Cotta–dk. |

Top Left Page 48	Top Center Page 50	Top Right Page 52
Middle Left Page 49	Middle Center Page 51	Middle Right Page 52
Bottom Left Page 53	Bottom Center Page 53	Bottom Right Page 53

Chart Diagram

Christmas Angel Top Left

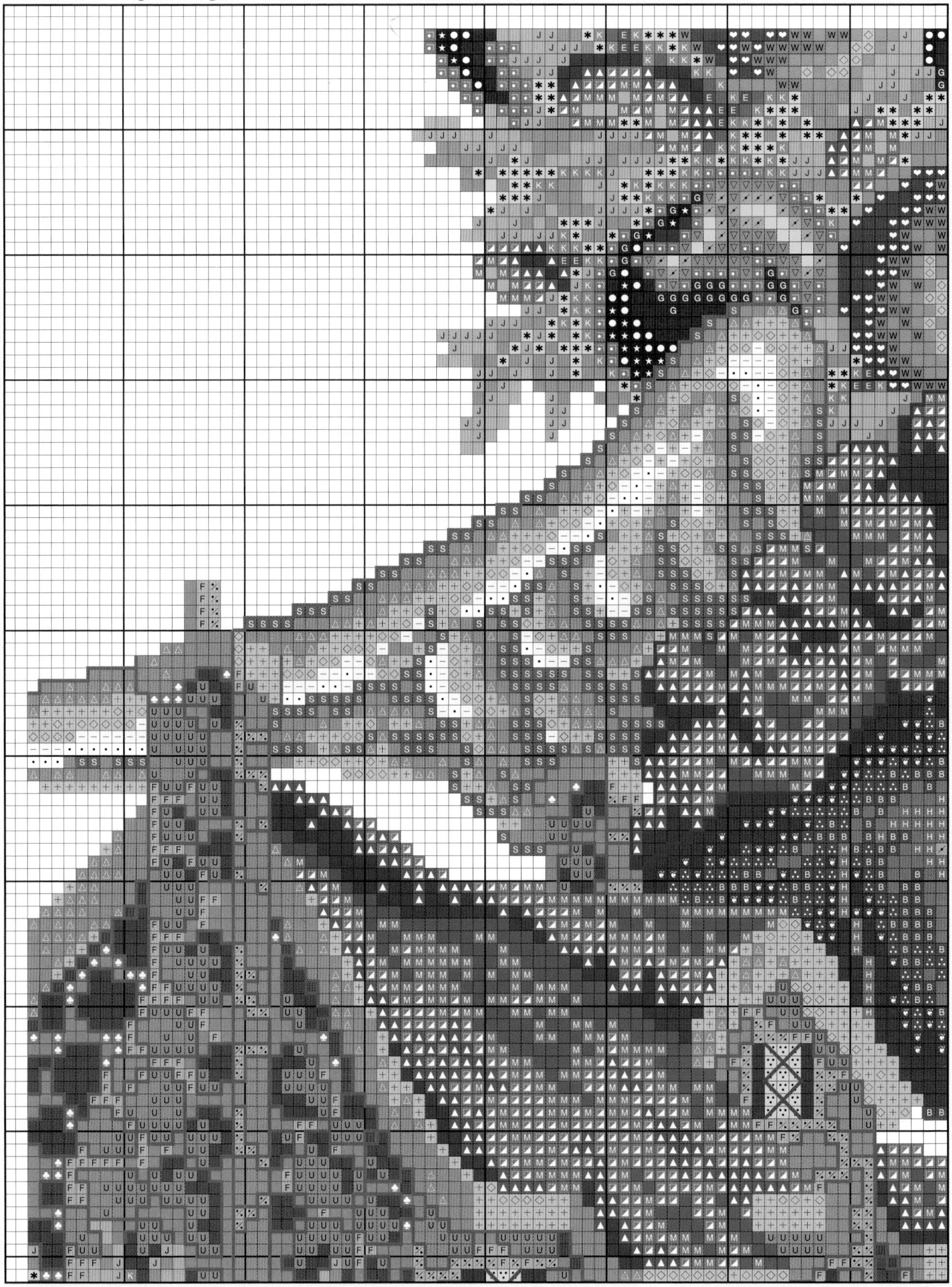

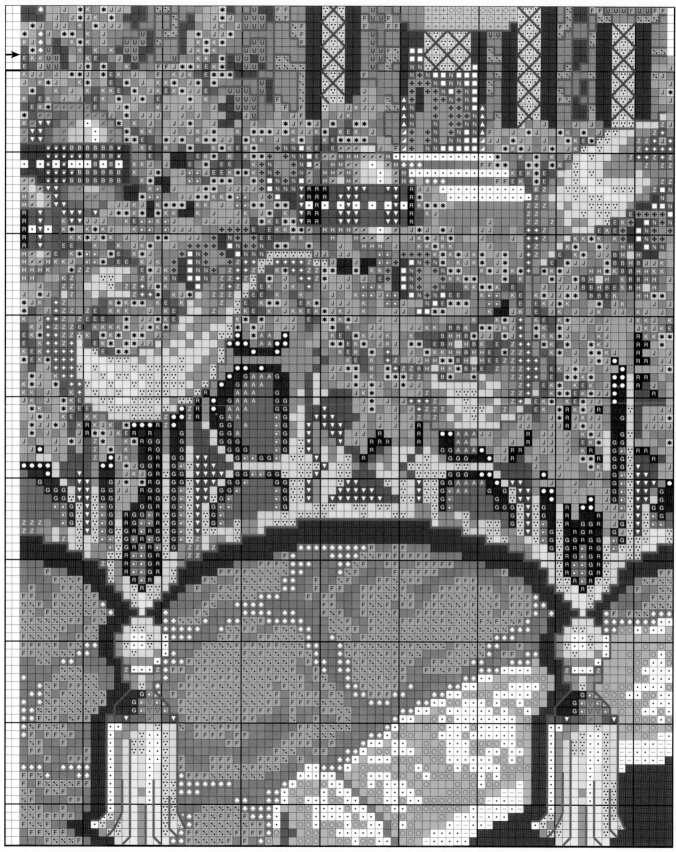

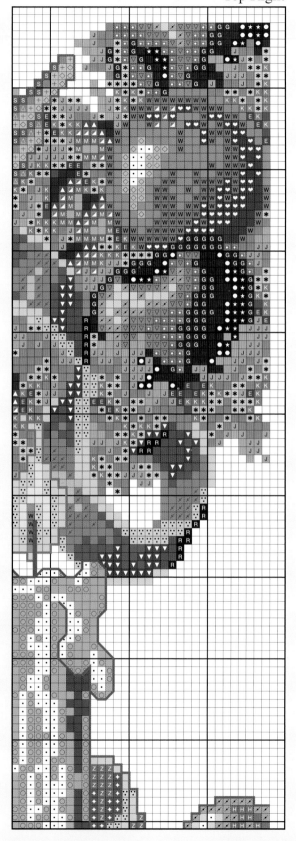

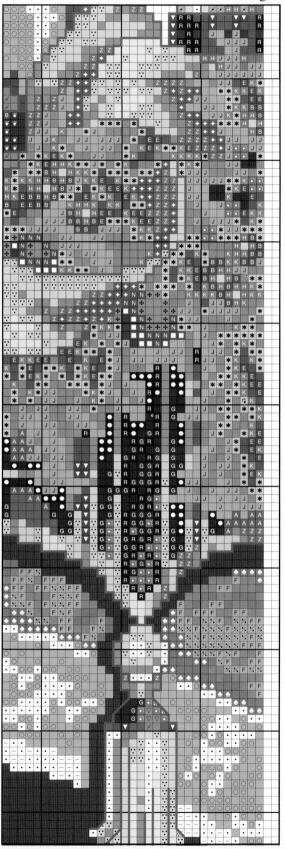

Bottom Left

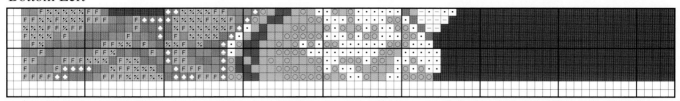

Bottom Center

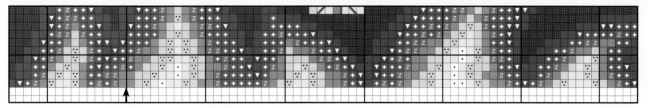

Bottom Right

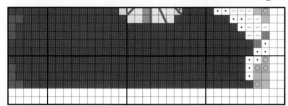

S t. Nick

Photo on page 54.

Materials
- Assorted trinkets
- Coordinating fabric: (½ yd.)
- Coordinating tassels: 2½"
  (2)
- Coordinating cording:
  ⅛"-wide (2 yds.)
- St. Nick: purchased 18"
  standing
- Tissue paper

General Supplies & Tools
- Coordinating thread
- Fabric scissors
- Hand-sewing needles
- Sewing machine

Note: A purchased St. Nick can be embellished with antique lace, and unique beads and other desired items to create that special touch.

Instructions
1. Cut a 16"-diameter circle from fabric. Fold edges under ½" and finger press. Fold under again ½" and sew to hem.

2. Sew a row of gathering stitches 1¼" from sewn edge. Sew a second row of gathering stitches 2" from sewn edge. Refer to Diagram 1. Pull gathers so fabric forms a sack.

Diagram 1

3. Stuff bottom of sack with tissue paper. Fill sack with trinkets.

4. Tack tassels onto ends of cording. Tie cording around sack and around arm of St. Nick. Fill sack with more trinkets if desired.

Sacred Sanctuary

Photo on page 55.

Materials

- Acrylic paints: dk. gold, dk. gray, off-white
- Acrylic sealer: matte
- Brass bell: ½"
- Clapboard siding: ¼" (3 sheets)
- Cross: small
- Door hinge assemblies (2)
- Eye screw: ½"
- Glass paints: blue, orange, purple, red, yellow
- Keyplate and door knob: 1/24 scale
- Permanent gold marker
- Sheets of glass: 9½" x 5" (2), 1½" x 3" (2), 1½" square
- Small gold chain: 1½"
- Texturizing gel
- Wood: balsa wood, 2" x 1⅞" x ¼"

Birch plywood or pine (Refer to page 6.)

Front, 9¾" x 5¼" x ½"
Back, 9¾" x 5¼" x ½"
Sides, 4¼" x 7⅜" x ½" (2)
Base, 9" x 12¾" x ½"
Roof, 11¾" x 3¼" x ½"
Roof, 11¾" x 3¾" x ½"
Vestibule front, 2¾" x 5¼" x ¼"
Vestibule sides, 2" x 2¾" x ¼" (2)
Vestibule way roof, 2⅝" x 2½" x ¼"
Vestibule way roof, 2⅝" x 2¾" x ¼"
Steeple walls (front and back), 1½" x 2½" x ¼" (2)
Steeple walls (side), 1⅛" x 1⅞" x ¼"(2)
Steeple roof, 1¼" x 2" x ¼"
Steeple roof, 1½" x 2" x ¼"

- Wooden chimney: 2" square x 3" high

General Supplies & Tools

- General Supplies & Tools on page 6.

Instructions

Refer to General Instructions for Angel House Construction pages 6-8. *Note: This angel house has been rotated so the front and back become the sides and the sides become the front and back.*

1. Cut wood for front, back, sides, and roof using table saw and patterns on page 59.

2. Cut wood for base using Base Pattern on page 58.

3. Cut wood for vestibule front, sides, and roof using Vestibule Patterns on page 58.

4. Cut wood for steeple walls and roof using dimensions given and Steeple Patterns on page 58.

5. Cut a "V" in bottom of wooden chimney to fit over 45° angle pitch of angel house roof using a jigsaw.

6. Transfer windows on sides of angel house using graphite paper and a stylus, and Sides Pattern on page 57. Transfer window of vestibule and window and door on front of vestibule using Vestibule Front Pattern on page 58.

7. Transfer openings in steeple walls using Steeple Patterns on page 58.

8. Drill pilot holes in each corner of windows and openings on steeple walls. *Note: All windows on sides of angel house and openings on steeple walls are arched at top. Windows on sides of vestibule are arched at top and bottom.*

9. Cut out window and door openings, using a jigsaw. Save door. Using a craft knife, cut ¼"-thick balsa wood piece into a door using saved door as pattern.

10. Assemble front, back, and sides of angel house and glue roof together using wood glue. *Note: Do not glue roof on at this time.*

11. Glue assembled angel house on base, aligning back and sides with outside edges of base.

12. Assemble front and sides of vestibule and glue roof together.

Note: Do not glue roof on at this time. Glue assembled vestibule to front of angel house and on base.

13. Assemble steeple and glue roof together. *Note: Do not glue roof on at this time.*

14. Apply texturizing gel in a circular motion to outside walls of angel house, vestibule, steeple, and chimney following manufacturer's instructions. *Note: Do not apply texturizing gel to top of chimney.*

15. Paint angel house, vestibule, and steeple on the inside with dark gold acrylic paint. Paint outside walls of angel house, vestibule, steeple, and chimney with off-white acrylic paint.

16. Paint top of chimney with dk. gray acrylic paint.

17. Spray angel house with matte acrylic sealer.

18. Randomly paint all sheets of glass to make stained glass windows, using blue, orange, purple, red, and yellow glass paints.

19. Attach sheets of glass over appropriate windows inside angel house and vestibule, using industrial-strength glue.

20. Glue clapboard siding to angel house, vestibule, and steeple roofs for shingles. Leave a ¼" overhang on angel house roof only.

21. Wash roofs on tops, bottoms, and all outside edges and front door on front, back, and all outside edges with dk. gray acrylic paint.

22. Carefully attach door to front of vestibule with door hinge assemblies using a dremel tool.

23. Attach keyplate and door knob to front side of door, using industrial-strength glue. Attach

cross above vestibule roof. See photo on page 55. Using a screwdriver, attach eye screw inside center of steeple roof. Hook chain to eye screw and brass bell to chain.

24. Attach roofs to angel house, vestibule, and steeple, using wood glue. Glue steeple centered on top of chimney and glue chimney 1⅛" in from front edge of angel house roof.

25. Write saying: *"Angelic Angels Praising Thee Within These Walls On Bended Knee,"* over the windows as shown in photo on page 55 using a permanent gold marker.

Sides Pattern   Enlarge 200%

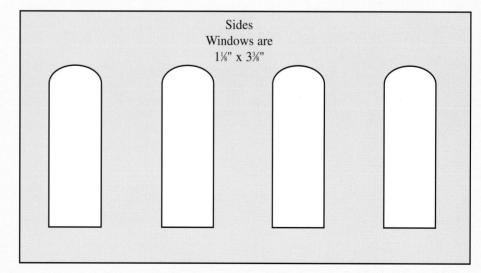

Sides
Windows are
1⅛" x 3⅜"

Base Pattern   Enlarge 200%

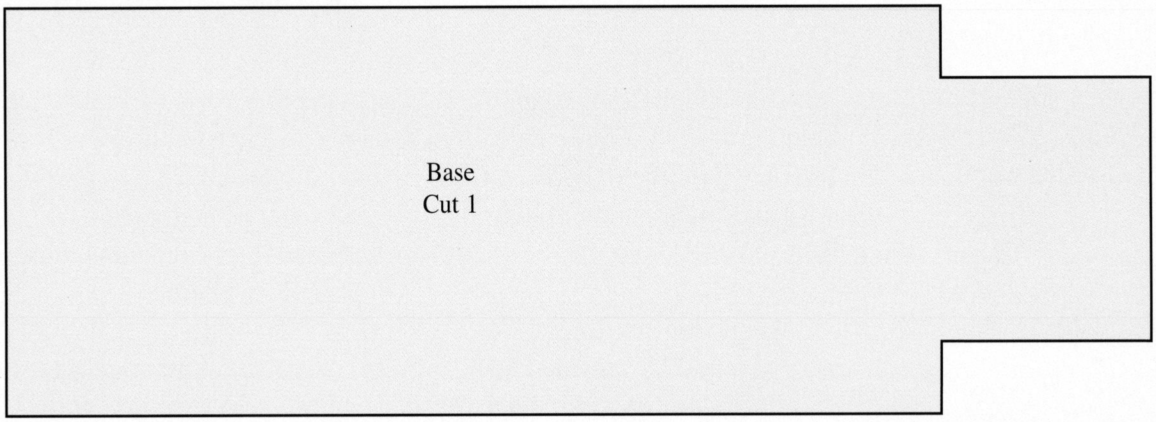

Base
Cut 1

Vestibule Front Pattern   Enlarge 200%

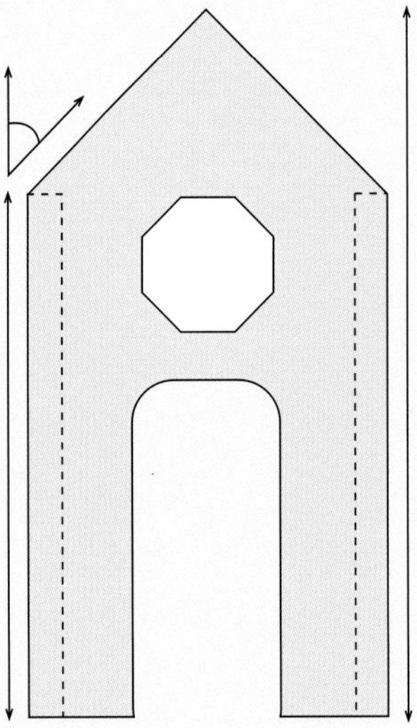

Front
2¾" x 5¼" x ¼"
Cut 1
Doorway is
1⅛" x 2½"
Octagonal
Window is
1" x 1"
Beginning at 3⅞",
cut pitch of roof
at 45° angle.

Vestibule Roof Pattern   Enlarge 200%

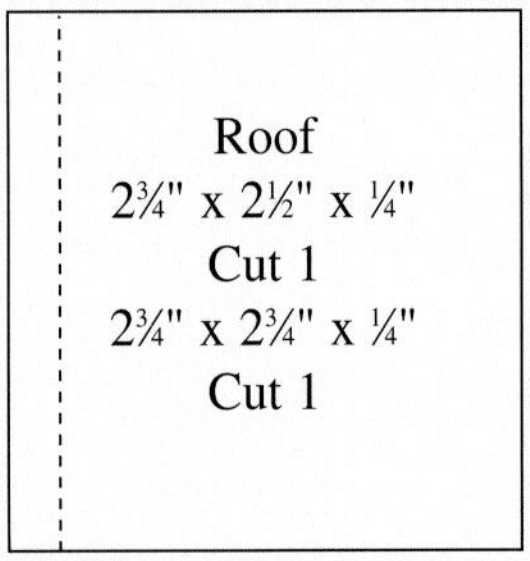

Roof
2¾" x 2½" x ¼"
Cut 1
2¾" x 2¾" x ¼"
Cut 1

Steeple Patterns   Actual Size

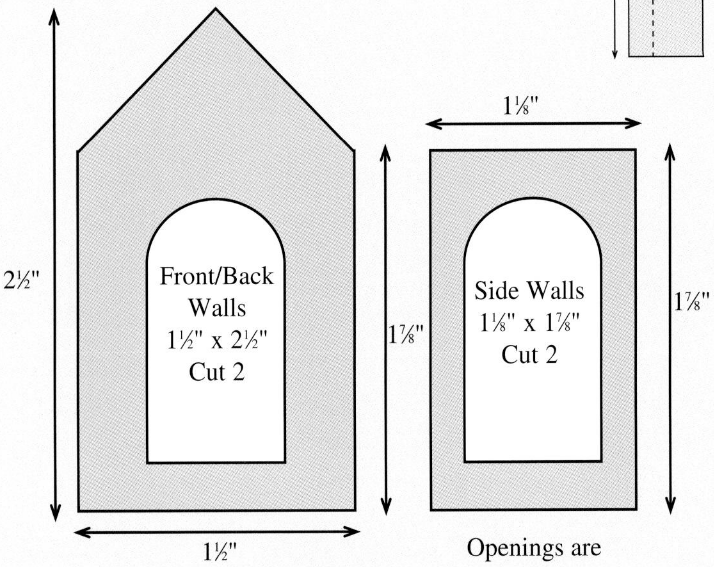

2½"

Front/Back
Walls
1½" x 2½"
Cut 2

1½"

Beginning at 1⅞", cut pitch of
roof at a 45° angle.
Openings are
¾" x 1⅜"

1⅛"

Side Walls
1⅛" x 1⅞"
Cut 2

1⅞"

1⅞"

Openings are
¾" x 1⅜"

Vestibule Sides Pattern   Enlarge 200%

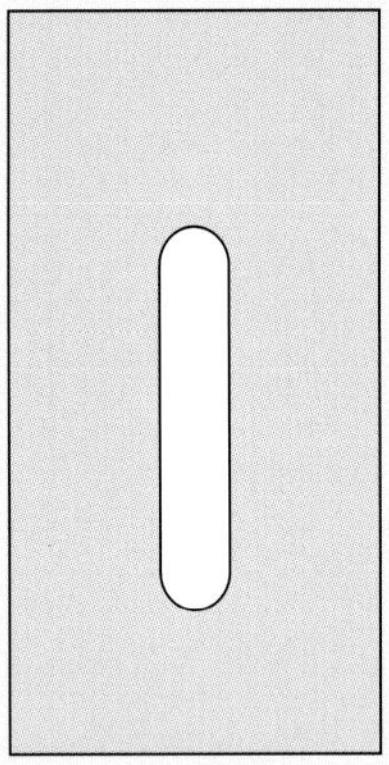

Sides
2" x 3⅞" x ¼"
Cut 2
Windows are
⅜" x 2"

Front and Back Pattern   Enlarge 200%

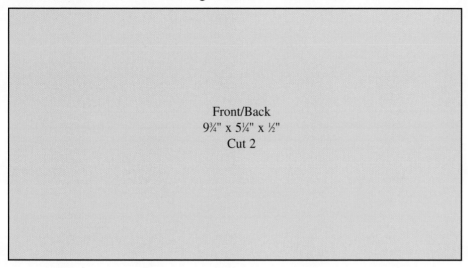

Front/Back
9¾" x 5¼" x ½"
Cut 2

Base Pattern   Enlarge 200%

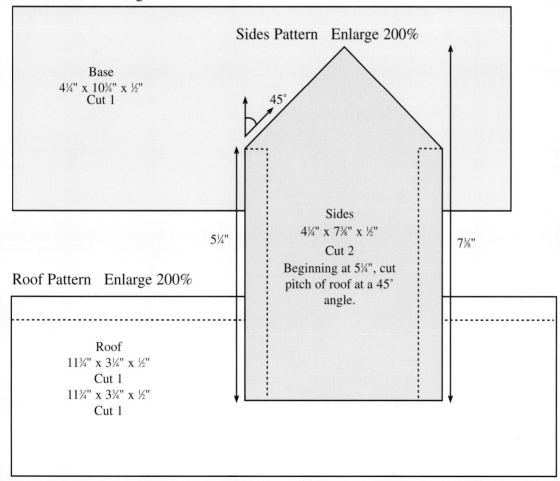

Base
4¼" x 10¾" x ½"
Cut 1

Sides Pattern   Enlarge 200%

45°

5¼"

7⅜"

Sides
4¼" x 7⅞" x ½"
Cut 2
Beginning at 5¼", cut
pitch of roof at a 45°
angle.

Roof Pattern   Enlarge 200%

Roof
11¾" x 3¼" x ½"
Cut 1
11¾" x 3¼" x ½"
Cut 1

Christmas Cottage

Materials

- Acrylic paints: antique gold, forest green, iron oxide, ivory, metallic gold
- Acrylic sealer: matte
- Christmas bulb garland: tiny
- Christmas wreath: tiny
- Cross: tiny
- Door hinge assemblies (4)
- Feather trees (2)
- Keyplates and door knobs: $\frac{1}{24}$ scale (2)
- Lace: 3"-wide off-white ($\frac{2}{3}$ yard)
- Lamp post: painted
- Star charm: tiny
- Wood: balsa wood: $\frac{1}{4}$" x 2" x 6";
- Wooden beads: small, large

Birch plywood or pine (Refer to page 6.)
- Front, $9\frac{3}{4}$" x $5\frac{1}{4}$" x $\frac{1}{2}$"
- Back, $9\frac{3}{4}$" x $5\frac{1}{4}$" x $\frac{1}{2}$"
- Sides, $4\frac{1}{4}$" x $7\frac{7}{8}$" x $\frac{1}{2}$" (2)
- Base, 9" x $12\frac{3}{4}$" x $\frac{1}{2}$"
- Roof, $11\frac{3}{4}$" x $3\frac{1}{4}$" x $\frac{1}{2}$"
- Roof, $11\frac{3}{4}$" x $3\frac{3}{4}$" x $\frac{1}{2}$"
- Entry way front, $2\frac{3}{4}$" x $4\frac{1}{8}$" x $\frac{1}{2}$"
- Entry way sides, 2" x $2\frac{3}{4}$" x $\frac{1}{2}$" (2)
- Entry way roof, $2\frac{3}{4}$" x $2\frac{1}{2}$" x $\frac{1}{2}$"
- Entry way roof, $2\frac{3}{4}$" x 3" x $\frac{1}{2}$"

General Supplies & Tools
- General Supplies & Tools on page 6

Instructions

Refer to General Instructions for Angel House Construction pages 6-8.

1. Cut wood for front, back, sides, and roof, using a table saw and patterns on page 59.

2. Cut wood for base using Base Pattern on page 58.

3. Cut wood for entry way roof using Entry Way Patterns on page 63.

4. Cut wood for entry way front and sides using altered dimensions given on pattern. Beginning at $2\frac{3}{4}$", cut pitch of roof at a 45° angle.

5. Transfer windows and doors on front, back, one side, and entry way front using graphite paper and a stylus and Window and Door Patterns on pages 62 and 64.

6. Drill pilot holes in each corner of windows. *Note: All windows are arched at top.*

7. Cut out windows and door openings, using a jigsaw. Save door. Using a craft knife, cut $\frac{1}{4}$"-thick balsa wood piece into a door using saved door as pattern.

8. Assemble front, back, and sides of angel house and glue roof together, using wood glue, *Note: Do not glue roof on at this time.*

9. Assemble front and sides of entry way and glue entry way roof together. *Note: Do not glue roof on at this time.* Glue assembled angel house on base, allowing $3\frac{3}{4}$" in front and 1" in back and on each side of base. Glue assembled entry way to front of angel house and on base using photograph on page 60 for placement.

10. Paint angel house and entry way on the inside and the outside with ivory acrylic paint.

11. Paint base, including all outside edges, with antique gold acrylic paint, then stipple top of base with ivory using an old paintbrush.

12. Paint both sides of angel house roof and entry way roof, including all outside edges; both sides of doors, including all outside edges; and all outside edges around base with forest green acrylic paint. Allow to dry. Paint shingles on roof using iron oxide acrylic paint and $\frac{1}{2}$"-wide flat paintbrush.

13. Paint bricks at each corner of angel house with iron oxide acrylic paint, leaving $\frac{1}{16}$-$\frac{1}{8}$" space

between each brick. Alternate position of bricks using photograph for placement.

14. Paint three horizontal bricks below each window with iron oxide, leaving $\frac{1}{16}$-$\frac{1}{8}$" space between each brick.

15. Paint five vertical bricks arched above each window and each door with iron oxide, leaving $\frac{1}{16}$-$\frac{1}{8}$" space between each brick. Make center brick slightly larger than others.

16. Paint bricks from front door angling outward toward right corner of base with iron oxide, alternating position of bricks in each row.

17. Draw a circle at least $\frac{1}{2}$" larger in diameter than base of lamp post, using a pencil. Paint bricks with iron oxide, keeping outer end of each brick even with pencil line.

18. Paint around each brick on the path and in the circle with ivory for mortar.

19. Using a ruler and a pencil, mark three horizontal placement lines on angel house roof and two horizontal placement lines on entry way roof. Allow approximately 1" between each placement line. Starting at bottom edges of roof lines and

working across, float-shade scallops with ivory. Alternate position of scallops on each row using photograph for placement.

20. Carefully attach doors to front and back of angel house with door hinge assemblies, using a dremel tool.

21. Adhere keyplates, and door knobs, to front sides of doors, using industrial-strength glue.

22. Cut lace into five 4" pieces, using fabric scissors. Attach lace to windows on inside of angel house to make curtains, using industrial-strength glue.

23. Using wood glue, attach roof on angel house. Attach roof on entry way.

24. Spray angel house with matte acrylic sealer.

25. Using industrial-strength glue, attach cross to front door. Glue each feather tree into wooden bead. Glue feather Christmas trees to right corner of angel house. Attach star charm to top of one feather tree.

26. Glue lamp post on base, centering in painted brick pattern. Glue Christmas wreath to lamp post.

Back Windows and Door Pattern   Enlarge 200%

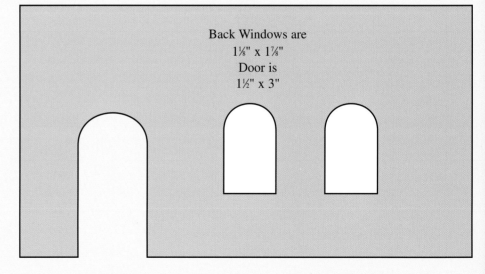

Back Windows are
$1\frac{1}{8}$" x $1\frac{7}{8}$"
Door is
$1\frac{1}{2}$" x 3"

Front Entry Way Pattern   Actual Size

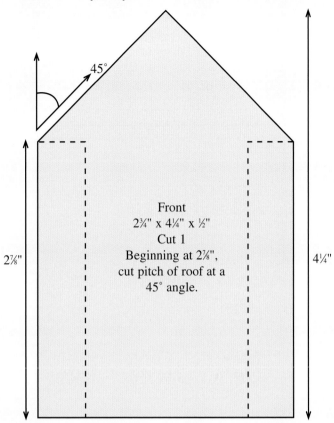

45°

2⅞"

Front
2¾" x 4¼" x ½"
Cut 1
Beginning at 2⅞",
cut pitch of roof at a
45° angle.

4¼"

Side Entry Way Pattern   Actual Size

Sides
2" x 2⅞" x ½"
Cut 2

Roof Entry Way Pattern   Actual Size

Roof
2¾" x 2½" x ½"
Cut 1
2¾" x 3" x ½"
Cut 1

Front Window Pattern   Enlarge 200%

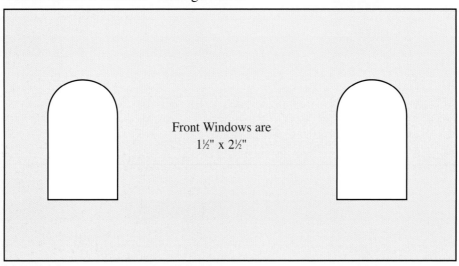

Front Windows are
1½" x 2½"

Side Window Pattern   Enlarge 200%

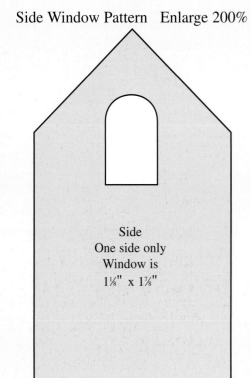

Side
One side only
Window is
1⅛" x 1⅞"

Entry Way Door Pattern   Actual Size

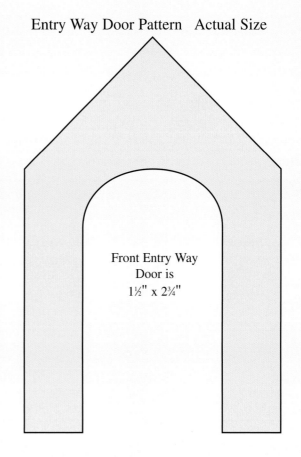

Front Entry Way
Door is
1½" x 2¾"

Celebrating Christmas Traditions

Chapter Two

eaded Nativity

Materials (for each)
- Perforated paper: 14 ct. cream
- Seed beads: Lt. Blue, Royal Blue, Bronze, Coral, Cream, Emerald, Garnet, Gold, Gray, Lt. Green, Christmas Green, Iris, Jet, Pale Peach, Christmas Red, Old Rose, Sapphire

General Supplies & Tools
- Beading needle
- Craft scissors
- Rubber cement
- Thread: coordinating; metallic gold

Instructions

1. For each ornament, cut perforated paper to size indicated. Bead each design following code at right and individual graphs on pages 67-72.

2. Cut out each design along heavy lines indicated on graph.

3. Refer to individual ornaments for finishing Loop Placement on pages 67-73.

4. With wrong sides facing and edges aligned, glue front design piece to back. For hanger, sew a 6" piece of metallic gold thread through top of ornament and knot ends together to make a loop.

Mill Hill Beads

Step 1: Beadwork

–	00123	Cream
	00148	Pale Peach
	00557	Gold
	00275	Coral
	00165	Christmas Red
	00553	Old Rose
	00367	Garnet
	00146	Lt. Blue
	00252	Iris
	00168	Sapphire
	00020	Royal Blue
	00525	Lt. Green
	00167	Christmas Green
	00332	Emerald
	00221	Bronze
	00150	Gray
	00081	Jet

Step 2: Cutting Line

Step 3: Loop Placement   See Instructions

Sample Information for Mary and Jesus, Joseph, Shepherd, and each Wise Man
Stitched on cream perforated paper 14 over 1. The finished design size is 1⅝" x 3¼". The paper was cut 4" x 6". Stitch one front and one back. Stitch count for each is 23 x 46.

Mary and Jesus
Begin loops for fringe by securing thread on back of design front at left bottom edge. Feed needle and thread through first symbol from back to front.

Mary and Jesus

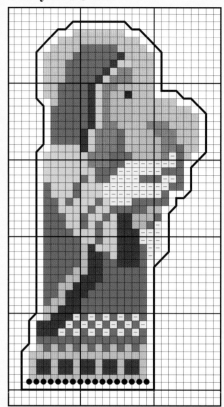

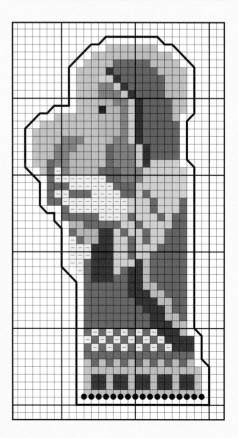

Joseph

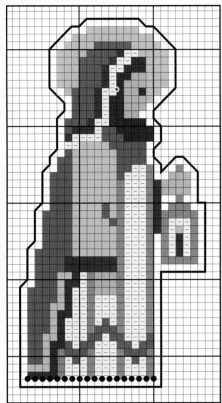

Shepherd

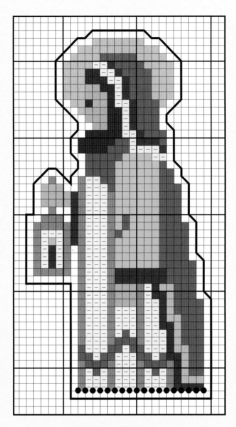

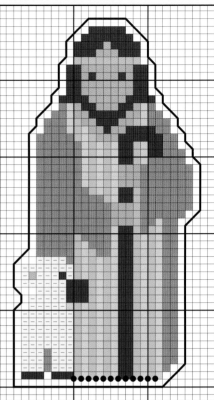

Thread five Iris, two Gold, one Garnet, two Gold, and five Iris beads; then feed needle and thread through next symbol from front to back. Repeat for seven more loops, securing thread on back. Repeat for design back.

Joseph

Begin loops for fringe by securing thread on back of design front at left bottom edge. Feed needle and thread through first symbol from back to front. Thread five Bronze, two Cream, one Emerald, two Cream, and five Bronze beads; then feed needle and thread through next symbol from front to back. Repeat for eight more loops, securing thread on back. Repeat for design back.

Shepherd

Begin loops for fringe by securing thread on back of design front at left bottom edge. Feed needle and thread through first symbol from back to front. Thread six Pale Peach, three Lt. Green, and six Pale Peach beads; then feed needle and thread through next symbol from front to back. Repeat for next five loops, securing thread on back. On design back, repeat for eight loops, each with six Bronze, three Pale Peach, and six Bronze beads.

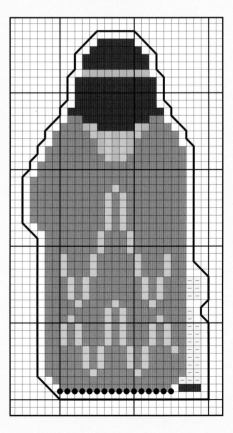

Green Wise Man

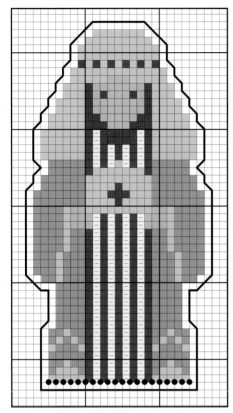 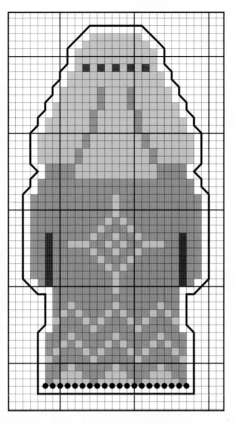

Pink Wise Man

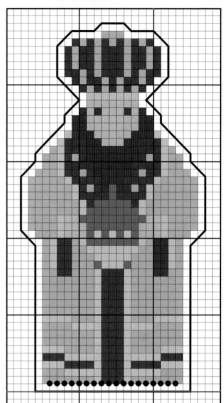

Green Wise Man

Begin loops for fringe by securing thread on back of design front at left bottom edge. Feed needle and thread through first symbol from back to front. Thread six Lt. Green, three Christmas Green, and six Lt. Green beads; then feed needle and thread through next symbol from front to back. Repeat for next two loops. For next four loops, thread each with 15 garnet beads. For last three loops, repeat first three loops, securing thread on back. On design back, repeat for ten loops, each with six Lt. Green, three Christmas Green, and six Lt. Green beads.

Pink Wise Man

Begin loops for fringe by securing thread on back of design front at left bottom edge. Feed needle and thread through first symbol from back to front. Thread five Old Rose, two Garnet, one Gold, two Garnet, and five Old Rose beads; then feed needle and thread through next symbol from front to back. Repeat for eight more loops, securing thread on back. Repeat for design back.

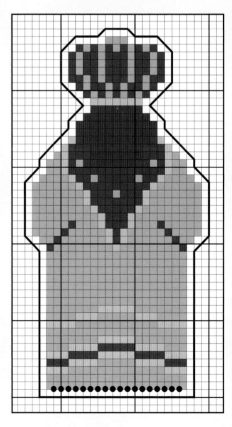

Blue Wise Man

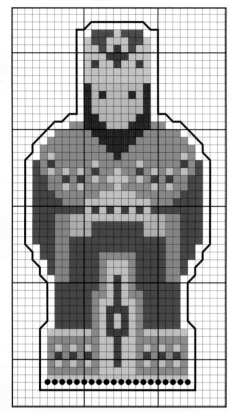

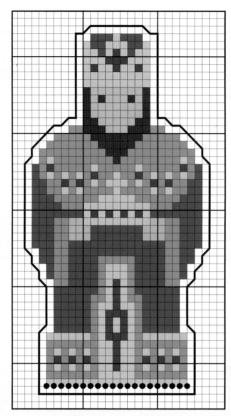

Complete directions before adding tail. To make tail, secure thread on one side of completed lamb at symbol, passing through lamb and exiting at symbol on other side. Thread 12 Cream beads and feed needle and thread again through lamb at same symbol. Secure thread and clip close to beadwork.

Lamb

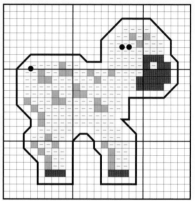

Blue Wise Man

Begin loops for fringe by securing thread on back of design front at left bottom edge. Feed needle and thread through first symbol from back to front. Thread six Royal Blue, three Gold, and six Royal Blue beads; then feed needle and thread through next symbol from front to back. Repeat for next three loops. For next two loops, thread each with six Garnet, three Gold, and six Garnet beads. For last four loops, repeat first four loops, securing thread on back. On design back, repeat for ten loops, three each with six Royal Blue, three Gold, and six Royal Blue beads.

Sample Information for Lamb

Stitched on cream perforated paper 14 over one, the finished design size is 1½" x 1½". The paper was cut 4" x 4". Stitch one front and one back. Stitch count is 21 x 21.

Lamb

Make ears by securing thread on back of design front at first symbol. Feed needle and thread through symbol from back to front. Thread 12 Cream beads; then feed needle and thread through next symbol from front to back, securing thread on back. On design back, repeat for other ear.

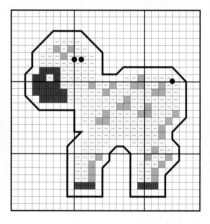

Sample Information for Angel

Stitched on cream perforated paper 14 over one, the finished design size is 1⅞" x 3¼". The paper was cut 4" x 6". Stitch one front and one back. Stitch count is 27 x 45.

Angel

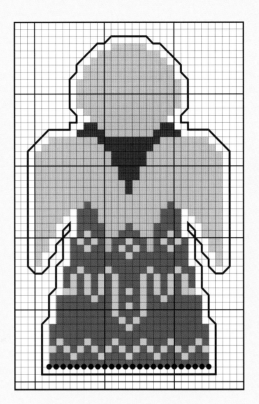

Angel

Begin loops for fringe by securing thread on back of design front at left bottom edge. Feed needle and thread through first symbol from back to front. Thread five Iris, two Lt. Blue, one Gold, two Lt. Blue, and five Iris beads; then feed needle and thread through next symbol from front to back. Repeat for next loop. For next eight loops thread each with five Lt. Blue, two Iris, one Gold, two Iris, and five Lt. Blue beads. For last two loops, repeat first two loops, securing thread on back. On design back, repeat for 12 loops, each with five Iris, two Lt. Blue, one Gold, two Lt. Blue, and five Iris beads.

Sample Information for Camel
Stitched on cream perforated paper 14 over one, the finished design size is 3⅛" x 3⅛". The paper was cut 6" x 6". Stitch one front and one back. Stitch count is 43 x 44.

Camel

Begin loops for blanket by securing thread on back of design front at left first symbol. Feed needle and thread through symbol from back to front. Thread five Lt. Green, one Christmas Red, one Christmas Green, one Christmas Red, and five Lt. Green beads; then feed needle and thread through next symbol from front to back, securing thread on back. Repeat for next two loops. On design back, repeat for three loops. Complete directions before adding tail. To make tail, secure thread on one side of completed

camel at symbol, passing through camel and exiting at symbol on other side. Thread 25 Bronze beads, make a loop with last six beads, and run needle back through first 19 beads. Feed needle and thread again through camel at same symbol. Secure thread and clip close to beadwork.

Sample Information for Donkey
Stitched on cream perforated paper 14 over one, the finished design size is 2⅞" x 3⅛". The paper was cut 5" x 6". Stitch one front and one back. Stitch count is 41 x 43.

Donkey

Begin loops for blanket by securing thread on back of design front at left first symbol. Feed needle and thread through symbol from back to front. Thread three Gold, one Garnet, and three Gold beads; then feed needle and thread through next symbol from front to back. For next two loops, repeat first loop, securing thread on back. On design back, repeat for three loops.

Continued on page 73.

Camel

Donkey

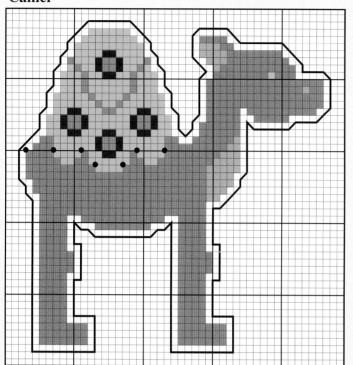

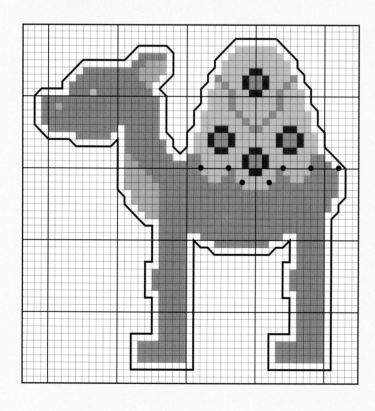

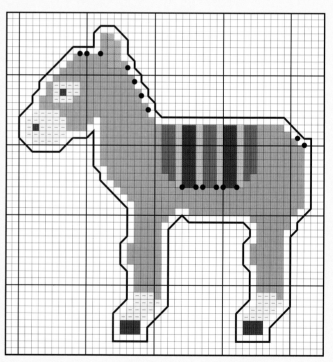

Continued from page 71.
To make mane, secure thread on back of design front at left edge of head. Feed needle and thread through first symbol from back to front. Thread 12 Jet beads; then feed needle and thread back through same symbol from front to back. Repeat for remaining six loops. On design back, repeat for seven loops. Complete directions before adding tail. To make tail, secure thread on one side of completed donkey at first symbol, passing through donkey and exiting at symbol on other side. Thread 34 Jet beads and feed needle and thread again through donkey at same symbol. Repeat for next loop, threading 24 Jet beads. Secure thread and clip close to beadwork.

Crèche
Materials
- Acrylic paints: dk. brown, golden brown, reddish brown, lt. yellow/gold
- Birch plywood: ¼"-thick (½ sheet)
- Fabric: brown board pattern (⅓ yd.)
- Liquid wood sealer
- Spray varnish
- Texture paste

General Supplies & Tools
- Fabric scissors
- Jigsaw
- Knives: craft; palette
- Paintbrushes: flat; old flat; large flat
- Paper palette: 9" x 12"
- Paper towels
- Plastic fork
- Sandpaper: med. grit
- Wood glue

Instructions
1. Enlarge and trace Back Wall/Filet Pattern on page 74 onto plywood. Cut out wall and filet using a jigsaw. Also cut plywood into the following sized pieces: 6" x 12" for base; two 5¼" x 9⅝" for roof angled and beveled at 30°; two 2¾" x 6¼" for side walls.

2. Refer to Diagram 1 and glue crèche together.

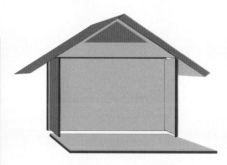

Diagram 1

3. Cut fabric slightly larger than inside and outside walls, filet front, and back wall. Apply a liberal amount of wood sealer to back wall of crèche using a large flat paintbrush. While sealer is wet, set fabric in place. Fabric will absorb excess sealer.

4. Brush over top of fabric to distribute sealer. If necessary, add more sealer to avoid any dry spots or puddles of sealer. Repeat process on inside and outside walls and front of filet. Allow to dry. Apply another coat of sealer to all fabric areas. When thoroughly dry, trim away excess fabric using a craft knife. Sand fabric until fabric feels smooth.

5. Refer to General Instructions for Texturizing Wood on page 16.

6. Pour a puddle of golden brown acrylic paint on palette paper. Thoroughly load a large flat paintbrush and paint roof, floor, and cut edges, making certain grooves are also covered. Allow to dry.

7. Pour a puddle of water on palette paper. Add reddish brown paint to water to create a transparent wash. Paint wash onto roof and floor, making certain grooves are also covered. Wipe off any excess color with a paper towel. Allow to dry.

8. Pour a puddle of lt. yellow/gold paint on palette paper. Stroke an old, flat paint-

brush through paint to load. Stroke paintbrush back and forth on a dry paper towel to remove excess paint. Stroke paintbrush over roof and floor in a slip-slap motion to highlight upper most portions of texture paste.

9. Pour a puddle of dk. brown paint on palette paper. Float around all outside edges of each fabric piece and cut edges of wood.

10. Spray crèche with several coats of varnish.

Back Wall/Filet Pattern Enlarge 320%

Gift Tags

Materials
- Cardstock: cream, tan, white
- Cording: ¹⁄₁₆"-wide metallic black rainbow
- Handmade papers: gray, green, red, tan, white
- #8 braid: metallic gold, metallic silver
- Raffia: natural (scrap)

General Supplies & Tools
- Craft glue
- Craft scissors
- Hand-sewing needles

Instructions
1. Cut cardstock into desired sizes for gift tags. Fold each gift tag in half.

2. Refer to photo and Diagram 1. Tear and cut coordinating hand-made papers into squares and crosses as shown. Accent crosses with stitches using a handsewing needle and metallic gold braid. Layer and glue squares, crosses, and raffia in place on tags.

Diagram 1

3. Stitch cording through top left corners of tags using a hand-sewing needle. Knot ends to create gift ties.

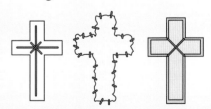

Optional Design Stitches

Created by Judi Kauffman

Stitched Bookmark

Photo on page 75.

Materials
- Braid: #4 gold; #16 metallic burgundy, gold
- Buttons: ¾" crystal (11)
- Embroidery floss: dusty blue, burgundy, gold
- Fray preventative
- Plastic canvas: 4" square 14-ct.
- Ribbon: metallic — 1/16"-wide gold, navy (⅜ yd.); grosgrain — ⅝"-wide navy (⅜ yd.)
- Ultra suede fabric: — 4" square burgundy

General Supplies & Tools
- Craft glue
- Craft scissors
- Tapestry needles: #22, #26

Instructions

1. Refer to stitch guide on right and Stitched Bookmark on page 77. Stitch cross onto plastic canvas using six strands of floss.

2. Cut out cross, leaving one row of plastic on all sides. Refer to General Instructions for Overcast Stitch on page 14. Overcast edges using metallic ribbons held at an angle for best coverage. If necessary, stitch two or three times in hole at outer corners to cover plastic.

3. Stitch buttons in place using #4 gold braid and smaller tapestry needle. Refer to Diagram 1 for direction of buttons.

Diagram 1

4. Cut backing from ultra suede using enlarged Cross Pattern. Glue one end of grosgrain ribbon to back of cross ½" below top edge. Glue backing to cross using a small amount of glue to prevent seepage to front. Treat other end of ribbon with fray preventative.

Cross Pattern   Enlarge 140%

Anchor		DMC	

Step 1: Continental Stitch (6 strands)

306		725	Topaz
20		498	Christmas Red–dk.
921		931	Antique Blue–med.
		202HL	Aztec Gold medium braid (1 strand)
		080HL	Garnet medium braid (1 strand)

Step 2: Whipstitch (1 strand)

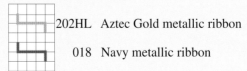

	202HL	Aztec Gold metallic ribbon
	018	Navy metallic ribbon

Step 3: Button Placement

Crystal Buttons (see diagram)

Stitched Bookmark

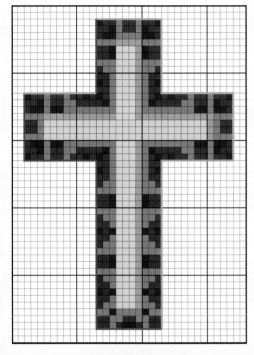

• Lightweight cardboard: scrap
• Pencil
• Scissors: craft; fabric

Yo-yo Cross

Photo on page 78.

Materials
• Fabric: as desired for mat cover (⅜ yd.); coordinating fabric scraps in shades of two complimentary colors
• Mat board: 10½" x 14"

General Supplies & Tools
• Compass
• Coordinating thread
• Craft glue
• Hand-sewing needles

Instructions

1. Draw a 2½"-diameter circle on cardboard scrap using a compass and pencil. Cut out circle using craft scissors to use as yo-yo pattern.

2. Trace yo-yo pattern onto fabric scraps and cut out using fabric scissors. Cut 60 circles from one fabric color for background and cut 57 circles from second fabric color for cross.

3. Refer to Diagram 1. Fold in edge of fabric circle ¼" and finger press.

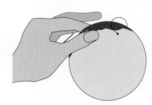

Diagram 1

4. Refer to Diagram 2. Sew a running stitch near folded edge using a hand-sewing needle and coordinating thread.

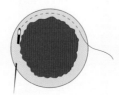

Diagram 2

5. Refer to Diagram 3. Gather edge and press flat with gathered edges centered. Secure ends of gathering threads and tuck inside yo-yo. Repeat process for all fabric circles.

Diagram 3

6. Cut mat cover fabric ½" larger than mat board. Cover mat board with fabric, wrapping and gluing excess fabric to back of board.

7. Arrange yo-yos in center of mat board as shown in photo on page 78. Glue yo-yos in place. Frame as desired.

Candle Lantern

Photo on page 79.
Materials
- Acrylic paints: dk. green, lt. green, med. green
- Enamel paints: dk. green, lt. green, red
- Jewelry: 2" cross
- Lantern: 9½" x 5½" stained glass
- Spray paint: bronze
- Wrapping paper: holly and berries

General Supplies & Tools
- Craft glue
- Craft scissors: small
- Découpage medium
- Paintbrushes: ¼"-flat; small, round
- Waxed paper

Instructions
1. Refer to photo on page 79 for placement. Dip tip of small round paintbrush handle in red enamel paint. Dot berries down sides of lantern.

2. Paint small comma stroke holly leaves between berries using lt. green enamel paint, and small round paintbrush. Paint over leaves using dk. green enamel paint in same manner as before.

3. Paint top of lantern using several shades of green acrylic paints and a ¼"-flat paintbrush. Using lt. green acrylic paint, stipple on top of lantern. Repeat process using med. green, then dk. green acrylic paints.

4. Cut out leaves and berries from wrapping paper. Paint découpage medium on backs of paper cut-outs and attach to top of lantern.

5. Paint edges of cut-outs using dk. green acrylic paint to blend with top of lantern.

6. Cover work surface with waxed paper. Lay top of lantern and cross on waxed paper and lightly spray with bronze paint.

7. Glue cross to front of lantern.

For unto you is born this day in the city of David a Saviour, which is Christ the Lord.
St. Luke 2:11

Magnetic Bookmarks

Photo on page 79.
Materials
- Greeting cards: as desired
- Magnetic sheet: adhesive-backed

General Supplies & Tools
- Craft scissors

Instructions
1. Cut greeting cards into 1¼-2" strips. Fold each strip in half.

2. Cut two small rectangles from magnetic strip to fit across bottom on front and back of each folded card strip. Remove paper backing from magnetic pieces and adhere to card strips.

Created by Randa Black

Flower Cards

Photo on page 81.

Materials

Wreath
- Acrylic paint: gold
- Cardstock: 8½" x 11" red; white
- Dried flowers: European sage sprigs; red verbena
- Glitter: gold
- Glitter spray
- Handmade paper: 4½" x 5½" white
- Pressed flowers: babies breath

Victorian Santa
- Cardstock: 8½" x 11" green
- Confetti: gold stars
- Handmade paper: 3" x 7" white
- Pressed flowers: red verbena; white bridal wreath
- Santa picture or photo

Christmas Rose
- Cardstock: 8½" x 11" cream; 4¼" x 5½" medium cream
- Glitter: gold
- Glitter spray
- Handmade paper: 6½" x 4½" white
- Pressed flowers: large rose petals; white larkspur; green larkspur sprigs
- Stencils: ½" alphabet

Instructions

Wreath

1. Cut red cardstock into a 10" x 7" rectangle using craft scissors. Fold in half to form a card.

2. Cut white cardstock into an 8" x 5" rectangle. Trim edges with decorative paper edgers. Paint edges of paper gold. Allow to dry, then fold paper in half. Glue paper 1¾" from top edge of card.

3. Write desired message or greeting using a marker on scrap of white cardstock. Outline letters with glue using a toothpick. Sprinkle letters with glitter and lightly blow excess glitter away. Cut out message using decorative paper edgers. Glue message inside card at top right side.

4. Cut handmade paper into a 4½" x 5½" rectangle. Spray all edges with water. Hold ruler along each edge and gently tear ¼" of paper away. Allow to dry.

5. Center and glue handmade paper to center front of card.

6. Lightly trace a 2½"-diameter circle in center of handmade paper. Glue sage sprigs to ¾-1½" and glue around circle to form a wreath. Glue verbena and baby's breath onto wreath.

7. Place card on newspaper. Spray glitter onto card front.

Victorian Santa

1. Cut green cardstock into a 10" x 7" rectangle and fold in half to form a card.

2. Center and glue handmade paper to front of card. Glue Santa picture to center of handmade paper.

3. Write desired message or greeting for front and inside of card using a marker on scrap of green cardstock. Cut out around messages using decorative paper edgers. Glue message to inside of card. Glue a large confetti star next to message. Glue remaining message at an angle above Santa picture on front of card.

4. Glue pressed flowers and confetti stars to front of card using a dab of glue on a toothpick.

5. Place card on newspaper. Spray glitter onto card front.

Christmas Rose Card

1. Cut cream cardstock into a 10" x 7" rectangle using craft scissors. Fold in half to form a card.

2. Beginning on right side, glue handmade paper to front of card.

3. Glue rose petals to top right of handmade paper to form a rose. Glue a thin stem below rose. Glue larkspur around stem.

4. Lightly stencil saying on half sheet of cardstock. Apply glue to letters using a toothpick. Sprinkle letters with gold glitter and lightly blow excess glitter away. Cut out around saying using decorative paper edgers. Glue saying to left front side of card.

5. Place card on newspaper. Spray glitter onto card front.

6. Glue a copy of The Legend of the Christmas Rose to inside of card.

The Legend of the Christmas Rose

Three Wise men had long been seeking a sign,
as they awaited the birth of the Christ child.
Finally, a very bright star appeared in the East
and they packed their gifts of gold,
frankincense, and myrrh, and traveled to
Bethlehem to a stable below the brilliant star.
A shepherd girl, seeing their glorious gifts, wept
because she had no gift to give the newborn King.
A passing angel saw her tears and where they had fallen
a beautiful white rose appeared.
The girl picked up the rose and followed the Wise men.
When she presented her gift, the Christ child smiled
and the petals of the rose turned red.

House Quilt

Photo on page 84.
Finished size: 25½" square.
Add ¼" to all quilt pieces for seam allowance.

Materials
- Fabrics: as desired; backing (¾ yd.)
- Quilt batting (¾ yd.)

General Supplies & Tools
- Dressmaker's pen: water-soluble
- Quilting needles
- Fabric scissors
- Sewing machine
- Thread: coordinating; contrasting

Instructions
Refer to quilting books for specific quilting techniques. Make this project into any desired size by adjusting House Quilt Templates accordingly.

1. Cut the following number of fabric pieces using the Enlarged House Quilt Templates on page 85: four of 1; one of 2; twenty-eight of 3; eight of 4; four of 5; four of 6; four of 7; sixteen of 8; eight of 9; four of 10, sixteen of 11; four of 12; four of 13; and four of 14.

2. Make quilt following House Quilt Diagram on page 86.

. . . choose you this day
whom ye will serve; . . . but as
for me and my house, we will
serve the Lord.
Joshua 24:15

House Quit Templates   Enlarge 160%

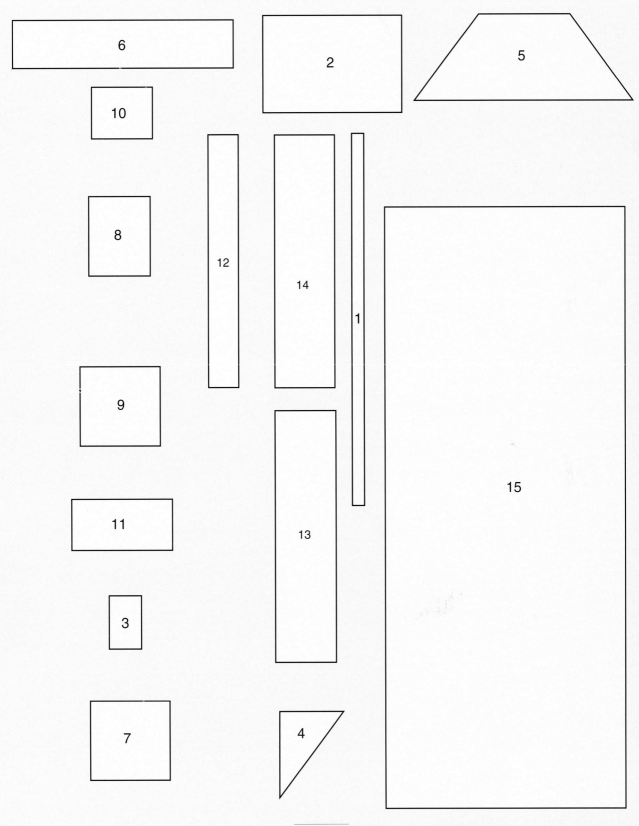

House Quilt Diagram

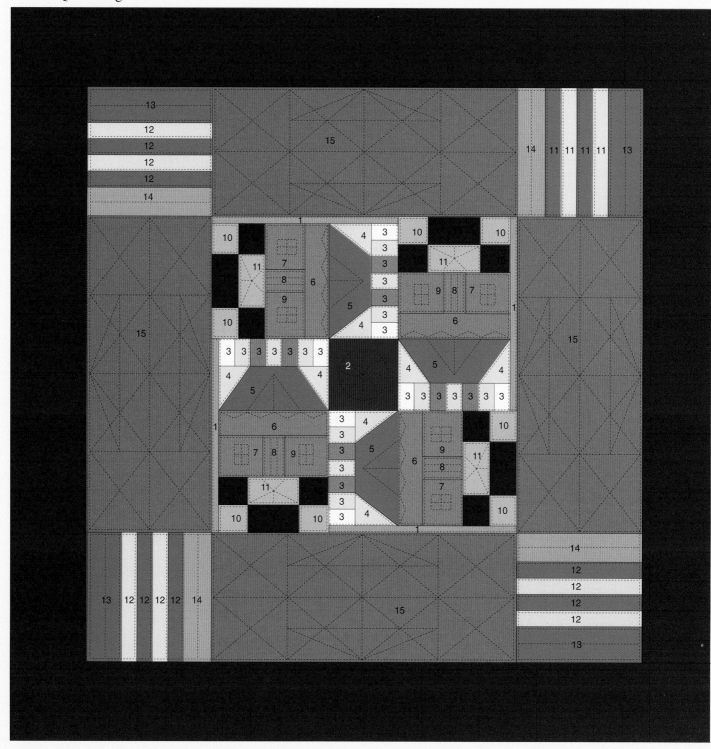

Star Quilt

Photo on page 87.
Finished size: 41" square.
Add ¼" to all quilt pieces for seam allowance.

Materials
- Fabrics: as desired; backing (1¼ yds.)
- Quilt batting (1¼ yds.)

General Supplies & Tools
- Dressmaker's pen: water soluble
- Fabric scissors
- Quilting needle
- Sewing machine
- Thread: coordinating; contrasting

Instructions
Refer to quilting books for specific quilting techniques. Make quilt into any desired size by adjusting Star Quilt Templates accordingly.

1. For outside stars, cut the following number of fabric pieces using enlarged Star Quilt Templates on page 89: twenty of 1 in one fabric; four of 1 in a second fabric; twelve of 2; nine of 3; eight of 4 and 5; twenty-four of 6; twelve of 8; eleven of 8 in coordinating fabrics; nine of 9; seventy-two of 15; and sixteen of 17.

2. For design #1, cut the following number of fabric pieces using the Star Quilt Templates: eight of 14 in one fabric; eight of 14 in a second fabric; four of 5, 7, 11, 19, and 21; and one of 8.

3. For design #2, cut the following number of fabric pieces using the Star Quilt Templates: four of 5, 7, 10, 12, 19, 21, and 22; eight of 14; and one of 18.

4. For design #3, cut the following number of fabric pieces using the Star Quilt Templates: four of 5, 7, 10, 12, 13, and 22; eight of 14; eight of 20; and one of 18.

5. For design #4, cut the following number of fabric pieces using the Star Quilt Templates: eight of 14 in one fabric; eight of 14 in a second fabric; four of 5, 7, 16, 19, 21, and 23; eight of 14; and one of 8.

6. Make quilt following Star Quilt Diagram on page 90.

Cathedral Quilt

Photo on page 91.
Finished size: 51" x 39".
Add ¼" to all quilt pieces for seam allowance.

Materials
- Fabrics: as desired; backing (2yds)
- Quilt batting (1½ yds.)

General Supplies & Tools
- Dressmaker's pen: water soluble
- Fabric scissors
- Quilting needle
- Sewing machine
- Thread: coordinating; contrasting

Instructions
Refer to quilting books for specific quilting techniques. Make quilt into any desired size by adjusting Cathedral Quilt Templates accordingly.

1. Cut the following number of fabric pieces using enlarged Cathedral Quilt Templates on page 92: two of 1, 2, 12, and 13; four of 3; forty-eight of 4; twenty of 5; twenty-eight of 6; eight of 7; twelve of 8; forty-eight of 9; thirty-two of 10; four of 11; sixteen of 14; one of 15; and twenty of 16.

2. Make quilt following Cathedral Quilt Diagram on page 93.

Star Quilt Templates   Enlarge 185%

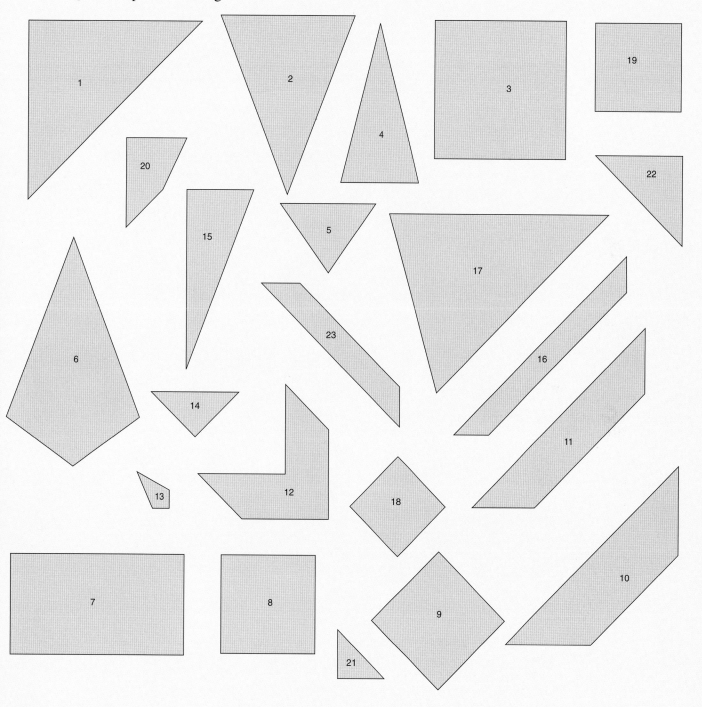

Star Quilt Diagram

Design #1

Design #3

Design #2

Design #4

Cathedral Quilt Templates   Enlarge 310%

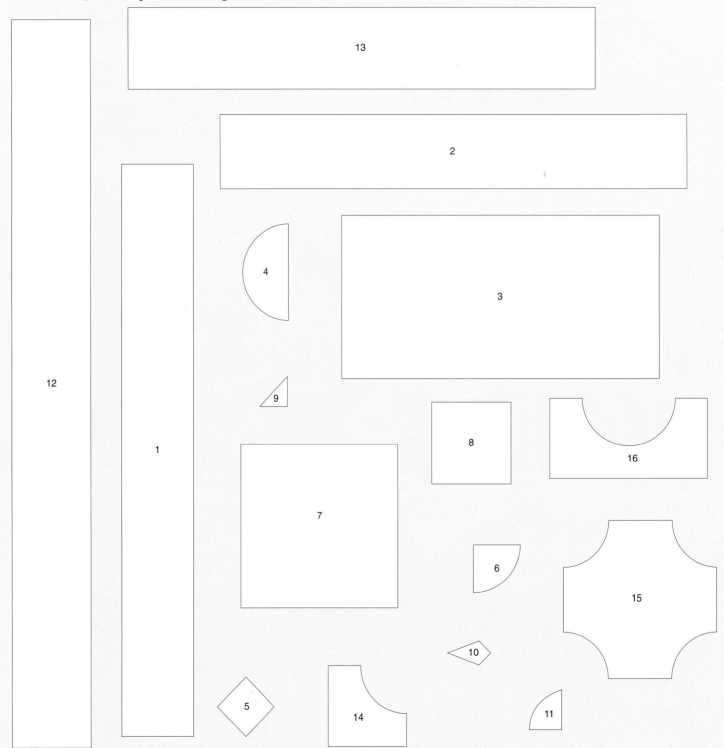

Cathedral Quilt Diagram (Diagram shown = ¼ of quilt — repeat three times.)

Sculpted Cherubs

Materials
- Acrylic paints: med. aqua, dk. brown, gray
- Acrylic sealer: matte
- Antiquing gel
- Cake decorating supplies: disposable bag; coupler; tip #61
- Crackle medium
- Joint compound: all-purpose(1 qt.)
- Plaster cherubs: 3½"-5" (3)
- Plywood tiles: ¾" x 8½" x 8½" (3)

General Supplies & Tools
- Butter knife
- Craft glue
- Oven
- Paintbrushes: ½" flat; small round; sponge

Instructions
1. Preheat oven to 190°.

2. Refer to photo for placement and glue cherubs to plywood tiles.

3. Refer to General Instructions for Joint Compound Application on page 10. Apply joint compound.

4. First make "C" shapes, then add leaves and dots. Make flower petals, then make the centers. When comfortable with process, make leaves and flowers on tiles.

5. To speed drying and cause crackling, place tiles in oven for 20 minutes, or until almost dry.

6. Randomly dab dk. brown paint onto tiles and cherubs. Allow to dry.

7. Using a sponge brush, apply crackle medium over dk. brown painted areas following manufacturer's instructions. Allow to dry.

8. Mix one tablespoon gray paint with one drop of med. aqua and paint tiles, allowing crackled areas to show through. Dilute paint with water and use a small round paintbrush to paint in the small cracks and crevices.

9. Dilute antiquing gel and lightly wash over tiles.

10. Spray tiles with matte acrylic sealer.

Gift Bag

Photo on page 96.

Materials
- Coordinating fabric: 5" x 7" scrap
- Double-sided adhesive sheet
- Gift bag with handle: 5½" x 7½"
- Handmade papers: assorted colors and textures (2)
- Lightweight cardboard: 4" x 7"
- Raffia: natural (½ yd.)

General Supplies & Tools
- Craft scissors
- Tracing paper

Instructions
1. Trace Cross Pattern on page 97 onto cardboard. Cut out pattern.

2. Cut a 5" x 7" rectangle from adhesive sheet. Attach adhesive to wrong side of fabric following manufacturer's instructions. Trace cross onto fabric adding ½" to all sides. Cut out cross. Remove paper backing from fabric cross and position on cardboard cross. Smooth fabric onto cardboard, wrapping excess fabric to back of cross. Continued on page 97.

Continued from page 95.
3. Attach adhesive to wrong side of handmade papers. Trace cross and a 1" x 6¼" strip onto one paper. Trace a 4½" x 5¼" rectangle and a 1¾" x 6¼" strip onto second paper. Cut out shapes and remove paper backing. Refer to photo for placement and press shapes in place.

4. Attach adhesive to back of fabric-covered cross. Trim excess adhesive from edges of cross. Remove paper backing and press cross in place.

5. Tie raffia into a bow around top of handles.

Cross Pattern   Actual Size

Keepsake Boxes

Photo on page 98.

Materials
- Acrylic gesso
- Acrylic paints: lt. gray, dk. mustard, burnt sienna, burnt umber
- Acrylic sealer: matte
- Bell: 2" brass
- Boxes: 4½" square wood with lids (2)
- Jewelry: 2½" cross
- Lightweight wire
- Macramé rings: 4" (2)
- Plastic leaf stem
- Spray paint: bronze metal

General Supplies & Tools
- Craft glue
- Glue gun and glue sticks
- Paintbrushes
- Sandpaper: medium grit
- Waxed paper
- Wire cutters

Instructions
1. Sand boxes. Remove all dust.

2. Apply acrylic gesso to boxes, then lightly sand again. Remove dust.

3. Paint boxes dk. mustard. Dilute burnt umber acrylic paint with water to create a dark wash. Paint circular shapes over all box surfaces.

4. Dilute burnt umber and burnt sienna acrylic paints with water and wash over boxes. *Note: To create the box on the right in the photo, dilute lt. gray acrylic paint with water and wash over box.*

5. Remove leaves from leaf stem. Cover work surface with waxed paper. Lay leaves, cross, bell, and macramé rings on waxed paper and spray with bronze metal paint, making certain to spray both front and back of all materials. Allow to dry, then lightly dab acrylic paints on all materials. *To create box on the right in the photo. Paint lt. gray wash over all items.*

6. Use a combination of craft glue and hot glue to attach macramé rings to center of box lids.

7. Refer to photo for placement and hot-glue leaves around base of rings.

8. Cut two 1" lengths from wire and use to attach cross and bell to top center of rings.

9. Spray boxes with matte acrylic sealer.

Beaded Rosary

Photo on page 100.

Materials
- Beads: amber oval glass (53); dk. brown oval glass (6); silver floral rondelles (24)
- Cross with loop
- Satin ribbon: ⅛"-wide green (3½ yds.)
- Virgin Mary charm with three loops

General Supplies & Tools
- Fabric scissors

Instructions
1. Cut a 48" length from ribbon. Tie a knot 8" from one end. String beads onto ribbon in following sequence: one silver rondelle, ten amber oval glass, and one silver rondelle. Tie a knot. Measure 1" and tie another knot, then string one silver rondelle, one dk. brown oval glass, and one silver rondelle. Tie a knot. Measure 1" and tie another knot. Repeat sequence three times, then end with one silver rondelle, ten amber oval glass, and one silver rondelle.

2. Tie ribbon ends onto charm, leaving 1" between charm and beads.

3. Tie remaining ribbon onto bottom of charm. Measure 1" from bottom of charm and tie a knot. String one silver rondelle, one dk. brown oval glass, and one silver rondelle. Tie a knot, then measure 1" and tie another knot. String one silver rondelle, three amber oval glass, and one silver rondelle. Tie a knot. Measure 1" and tie cross onto ribbon. Cut excess ribbon from knot.

Divine Bookmarks

Photo on page 102.

Materials
Pearls & Lace Bookmark
- Beads, white pearl: extra small (5); small (15); medium (13); large (9)
- Lace: ¾"-wide flat ecru (⅞ yd.)
- Wire, silver: 24 gauge (⅜ yd.); 28 gauge (2")

Purple & Green Beaded Bookmark
- Beads: assorted shapes and sizes of green, purple, silver (10 total)
- Cross charm: ¾" silver
- Jump ring: ³⁄₁₆" silver
- Overdyed yarn: green/purple variegated (2¼ yds)
- Wire: 20 gauge silver (⅜ yd.)

Cross Bookmark
- Cross charm: 2½" gold
- Necklace clasp: ³⁄₁₆" gold
- Ribbon: 1½"-wide taupe with gold edges (⅞ yd.)

General Supplies & Tools
- Craft glue
- Fabric scissors
- Needlenose pliers
- Wire cutters

Instructions
Pearls & Lace Bookmark
1. Fold lace in half matching ends. Tie an overhand knot about 2½" from loose ends. Set aside.

2. Cut a 12" length from 24 gauge wire using wire cutters. Refer to Diagram 1 and thread beads onto wire. Attach end beads to wire using craft glue. Continued on page 101.

Continued on page 101.

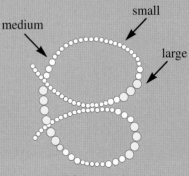

medium   small   large

Diagram 1

Continued from page 99.

3. Cut 28 gauge wire in half. Loop one wire around top of beaded letter and twist to attach to looped end of lace. Trim ends of wire. Thread five extra small beads onto remaining wire. Wrap beaded wire around lace just below knot. Twist ends of wire together and trim.

Purple & Green Beaded Bookmark

1. Cut a 12" length from wire using wire cutters. Thread assorted beads onto wire as desired. Beads should span a 3-3½" length at center of wire.

2. Refer to Diagram 2. Using needlenose pliers, bend wire into a small loop about 4" from end of wire to anchor bottom beads. Curl end of wire. Form a ½" loop at top of beads, then wrap wire around base of loop to secure. Bend wire down and out, then curl.

Diagram 2

3. Attach cross charm to jump ring using a small piece of wire.

4. Cut four 20" strands of yarn. Thread ends through jump ring. Attach a small bead onto yarn 2" away from ends. Tie an overhand knot 1½" from end and slip ring up to base of knot.

5. Refer to Diagram 3 and insert folded end of yarn through top loop of beaded wire. Separate strands to make a loop and feed knotted end of yarn through loop and pull tight to secure yarn to wire.

Diagram 3

Cross Bookmark

1. Attach cross charm onto necklace clasp.

2. Fold ribbon in half matching ends. Slip ribbon through clasp and tie an overhand knot 3" from ends. Cut ends of ribbon at an angle using fabric scissors.

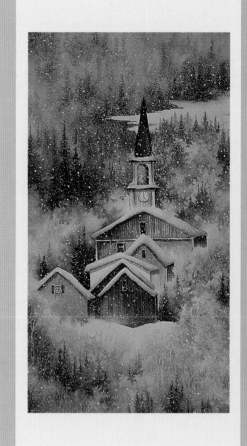

*And suddenly there was . . .
a multitude of heavenly hosts
praising God, and saying,
Glory to God in the highest,
and on Earth peace,
good will toward men.*
St. Luke 2:13-14

Cross Ornaments

Photo on page 104.

Materials
- Braid: #8 blue, lavender, rose
- Coordinating beads: antique glass seed; vintage faceted
- Embroidery floss: lt. green, variegated green, variegated gray-green, lavender, lt. lavender, variegated lavender-teal, dk. mauve, variegated mauve-tan, variegated peach, lt. pink, variegated pink-gray, teal
- Fabric: 6" x 4" black ultra suede
- Plastic canvas: 8½" x 11" 14-ct.

General Supplies & Tools
- Coordinating thread
- Craft glue
- Needles: beading; tapestry #26
- Scissors: craft; fabric

Instructions
1. Refer to stitch guide and Cross on page 105. Stitch crosses onto plastic canvas using six strands of floss.

2. Cut out three crosses using craft scissors and leaving one row of plastic on all sides.

Refer to General Instructions for Overcast Stitch on page 14. Overcast edges on Cross 1 using variegated peach floss held at an angle for best coverage. If necessary, stitch two or three times in hole at outer corners to cover canvas. Overcast edges on Cross 2 using lt. lavender floss. Overcast edges on Cross 3 using lt. pink.

3. Refer to Crosses 1, 2, and 3 below for placement. Stitch beads in place using a beading needle and coordinating thread.

4. Trace three crosses onto ultra suede and cut out slightly smaller than traced line using fabric scissors. Glue fabric crosses onto back of plastic canvas crosses.

5. Cut a 10" length from each braid. Fold one braid in half and tack ends to a coordinating cross for hanger. Repeat process using remaining braids and crosses.

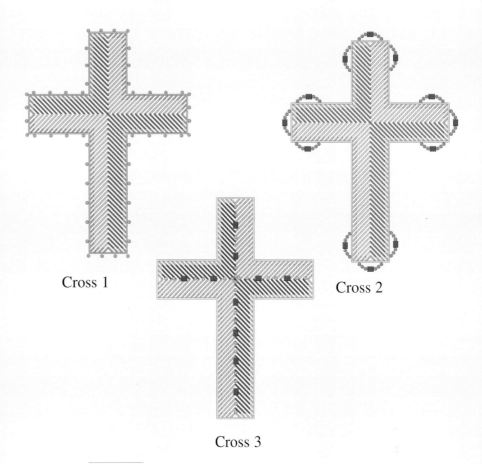

Cross 1

Cross 2

Cross 3

Cross Ornament #1

Anchor   **DMC**

Step 1: Satin Stitch (6 strands)

851   924   Slate Green–vy. dk.

        Variegated Violet to Blue Overdyed Floss

Step 2: Continental Stitch (6 strands)

870   3042   Antique Violet–lt.

Step 3: Bead Placement

   03037   Abalone (see diagram)

Cross

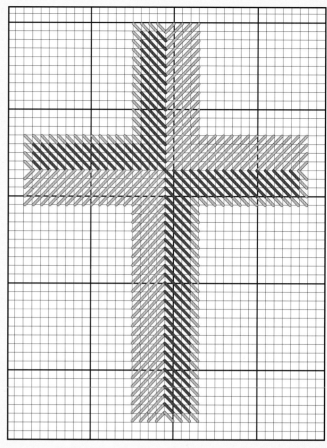

Cross Ornament #2

Anchor   **DMC**

Step 1: Satin Stitch (6 strands)

860   3053   Green Gray

        Variegated Green to Gray Overdyed Floss

Step 2: Continental Stitch (6 strands)

        Variegated Green Overdyed Floss

Step 3: Bead Placement

   03036   Cognac (see diagram)

        Vintage Beads (see diagram)

Cross Ornament #3

Anchor   **DMC**

Step 1: Satin Stitch (6 strands)

69   3687   Mauve

        Variegated Mauve to Gray Overdyed Floss

Step 2: Continental Stitch (6 strands)

        Variegated Rose to Tan Overdyed Floss

Step 3: Bead Placement

   03023   Platinim Violet (see diagram)

        Vintage Beads (see diagram)

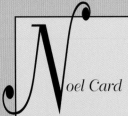

Noel Card

Photo on page 104.

Materials
- Braid: #8 confetti pink (1 yd.)
- Double-sided adhesive sheets
- Handmade papers: five assorted coordinating colors
- Lightweight mat board: 15" x 4" beige

General Supplies & Tools
- Craft glue
- Craft knife
- Craft scissors
- Hand-sewing needles

Instructions

1. Refer to Envelope/Lining Pattern on right. Trace enlarged Envelope/Lining Pattern onto desired handmade papers. Cut out patterns using craft scissors.

2. Glue lining to inside of envelope as shown in Diagram A on right. Beginning with side tabs, fold envelope as indicated. Glue back of envelope to tabs.

3. Cut six small embellishments in rectangle shapes. Dampen one end of three rectangles with water and gently tear away. Refer to Diagram B on page 107. Glue

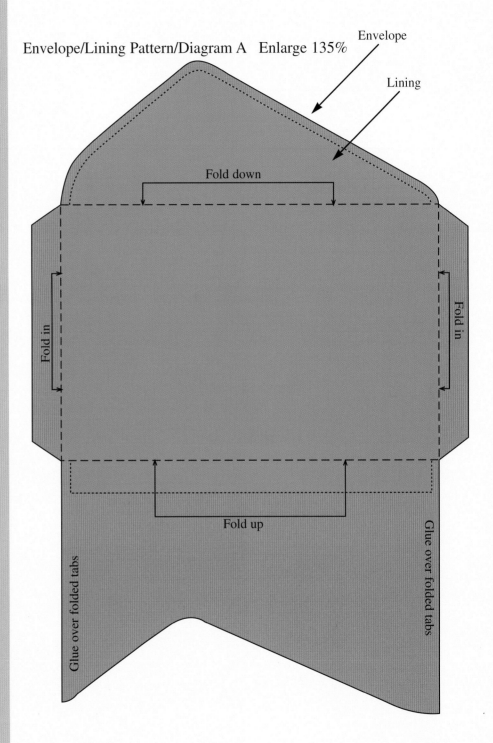

Envelope/Lining Pattern/Diagram A   Enlarge 135%

Envelope

Lining

Fold down

Fold in

Fold in

Fold up

Glue over folded tabs

Glue over folded tabs

rectangles to envelope. Set aside other three rectangles.

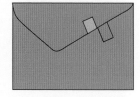

Diagram B

4. Refer to Diagram C. Fold mat board every 3" creating five folds. Score mat board on folds using a craft knife. Cut five 3" x

2½" rectangles out of handmade paper of choice.

Diagram C

5. Attach double-sided adhesive sheets to wrong side of handmade papers following manufacturer's instructions. Refer to photo for placement.

6. Refer to Letter Pattern below and trace patterns onto desired papers. Leave ½" along one side of paper designated for letter "E" and small rectangles free of adhesive to enable tearing.

Dampen points of "E" and one end on three remaining rectangles with water and gently tear away. Cut out patterns and remove paper backing using craft scissors. Press rectangles and letters in place on mat board.

7. Stitch stripes onto letters and shapes as shown using a hand-sewing needle and braid.

8. Fold card and slip into envelope.

Letter Pattern   Enlarge 110%

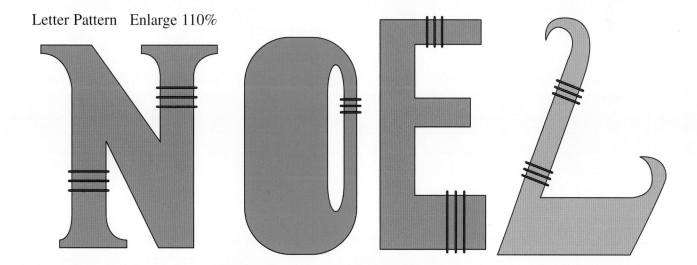

Lace Bible Cover

Model size is 8" x 5½".
Materials
- Beads: vintage pearl (4); champagne petite seed (1 pkg.); silver vintage seed (18)
- Buttons: ¼" vintage pearl (4)
- Fabric: moiré — 10" x 15" peach; sueded silk — 10" x 15" pale yellow; Damask — 3½" x 20" off-white
- Lace: 3-9" assorted ivory and ecru vintage pieces (8-9)
- Lightweight cardboard: 8" x 22"
- Quilt batting: 5½" x 8½"
- Ribbon: silk — 4mm ivory (¼ yd.); pale peach (½ yd.); blush, ecru, dk. ecru, pale gold, white (¾ yd. each); velvet — ³⁄₁₆"-wide ivory (2 yds.)
- Trim: ⅜"-wide ivory lace (⅞ yd.)

General Supplies & Tools
(for all bible covers)
- Coordinating thread
- Craft glue: thin-bodied
- Fabric scissors
- Glue gun and glue sticks
- Iron and ironing board

- Needles: beading; # 3 embroidery; hand-sewing
- Paint roller with tray: 3" disposable
- Paper bag: brown
- Rags: wet; dry

Instructions
Refer to General Instructions on pages 8-16 for Bible Cover Assembling and for ribbon work and stitches that are used for this project.

1. Cut cardboard.

2. Cut silk fabric for inner pocket front and inner pocket back. Cut moiré fabric for front and back. Cut Damask fabric for spine.

3. Press vintage laces. Pin laces to front and back moiré fabrics, overlapping laces ¼". Use curved lace pieces for bridging gaps along outer edges. Whip-stitch lace pieces to fabric using a hand-sewing needle and co-ordinating thread. Press as needed.

4. Cut white, blush, pale gold, ecru, and dk. ecru silk ribbons into two 5" lengths each. Cut ivory silk ribbon into one 5" length. Stitch each ribbon into a Rosette. Randomly place and hand-stitch rosettes to lace. Cascade pale peach silk ribbon around rosettes. Tack cascaded ribbon to lace with seed beads. Cluster and hand-stitch beads and buttons to lace.

5. Assemble spine.

6. Assemble bible cover. Flute underside of back with velvet ribbon. With wrong sides together, glue back to inner pocket back. Glue edge of lace trim to underside edge of front. With wrong sides together, glue front to inner pocket front. Hold remaining silk ribbon lengths together as one. Glue one end to inside spine of bible. Drape ribbons through bible pages. Knot ribbon ends.

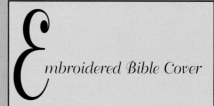

Embroidered Bible Cover

Photo on page 110.
Model size is 6" x 8¾".
Ribbons are hand-dyed for this project.
Materials
- Embroidery floss: khaki brown, lt. brown (½ yd. each)
- Fabric: 10" x 8" khaki green silk charmeuse; 44"-wide purple crushed velvet (¼ yd.)

Continued on page 111.

Created by Mary Jo Hiney

Continued from page 109.
- Lace: ¼"-wide gold metallic (⅞ yd.)
- Lightweight cardboard: 24" x 8¼"
- Blender pens: waterbased dual-tip med. blue, blush, lt. brown, med. brown, burgundy, dk. burgundy, lt. gray, med. gray, dk. green, med. green, peach, bright pink, lt. pink, med. pink, dk. purple, dk. yellow-brown, lt. yellow-brown, yellow-gold, dk. yellow-gold
- Quilt batting: 6" x 9¼"
- Ribbon: silk — 4mm purplish-gray (4½ yds.); brown (3½ yds.); dk. green (2 yds.); lt. green (3 yds.); olive green (2 yds.); khaki green (2 yds.); lt. rose (3 yds.); pale yellow (6 yds.); white (6 yds.); taffeta — 1"-wide khaki green (½ yd.)
- Trim: ¼"-wide purple/green buds and bow garland (⅞ yd.)

Additional General Supplies & Tools
- General Supplies & Tools on page 109
- Embroidery frame
- Paper towels
- Plastic cups (6)
- Salt

Instructions
Refer to General Instructions on pages 8-16 for Bible Cover

Assembling and for ribbon work and stitches that are used for this project.

1. Cut cardboard.

2. Cut velvet fabric for inner pocket front, inner pocket back, and back.

3. Cut silk charmeuse fabric 2" larger all around for front.

4. Cut velvet fabric for spine.

5. Cut white and pale yellow silk ribbons in half. Fill plastic cups halfway with cold water. Pour ¼ cup salt into each cup and dissolve salt. Place lt. green, lt. rose, and each 3 yd. length of white and pale yellow silk ribbon into each cup. Allow to soak for ten minutes.

6. Place paper towels on work surface. Remove lt. green ribbon from cup. Squeeze liquid from ribbon, open up, and lay flat on paper towel. Immediately dye ribbon using med. green, med. blue, dk. green, and lt. and dk. yellow-brown pens to make green hand-dyed ribbon. Begin dying ribbon using first shade of pen, skipping it along the ribbon and leaving space for the other shades. Repeat with remaining pen shades. Lightly coat entire ribbon with pens. Set ribbon

aside on paper towel to dry for ten minutes. Repeat process until all six ribbons have been dyed. Dye lt. rose ribbon using blush, lt. gray, med. gray, and lt. pink pens to make blush hand-dyed ribbon. Dye one white ribbon using bright pink, med. pink, burgundy, and dk. yellow-brown pens to make bright pink hand-dyed ribbon. Dye second white ribbon using med. brown, dk. burgundy, dk. purple, and dk. yellow-brown pens to make purple hand-dyed ribbon. Dye one pale yellow ribbon using bright pink, med. pink, burgundy, and dk. yellow-brown pens to make bright rose hand-dyed ribbon. Dye second pale yellow ribbon using peach, lt. gray, yellow-gold, and dk. yellow-gold pens to make gold hand-dyed ribbon.

7. Place all six shades of ribbons back in the six cups of salted water and soak for five minutes. Rinse each shade in fresh, cold water until color runs clear. Squeeze liquid from ribbon. Set hand-dyed ribbons aside on paper towels. Allow to dry for 15 minutes. Press with hot iron.

8. Place front fabric in embroidery frame. Use enlarged Transfer Pattern on page 112 to transfer design to center of fabric. Embroider fabric following Stitch Guide on page 113.

9. Remove fabric from frame. Trim fabric to ¾" larger than cardboard.

10. Assemble spine.

11. Assemble bible cover. Glue edge of lace to underside of back. With wrong sides together, glue back to inner pocket back. With wrong sides together, glue front to inner pocket front. Glue trim to outer edge of front. Glue one end of taffeta ribbon to inside spine of bible. Drape ribbon through bible page. Knot ribbon end.

Transfer Pattern   Enlarge 130%

Stitch Guide

Description	Ribbon/Floss	Stitch
1. Wisteria stems	lt. brown floss (2 strands)	Outline Stitch
2. Leaf spray stems	khaki brown floss (2 strands)	Outline Stitch
3. Wisteria	purple hand-dyed, purple-gray, brown	Lazy Daisy Stitch
4. Wisteria	purple hand-dyed, purple-gray, brown	Ribbon Stitch
		Ribbon Stitch, 1-twist
5. Daisy	gold, blush, bright rose, bright pink hand-dyed	Knotted and Looped
		Ribbon Stitch
6. Leaf spray leaves	green hand-dyed, lt. green, dk. green	Cross-over Lazy
		Daisy Stitch
7. Leaves	green hand-dyed, khaki green	Ribbon Stitch, 1-twist

Stitch Guide

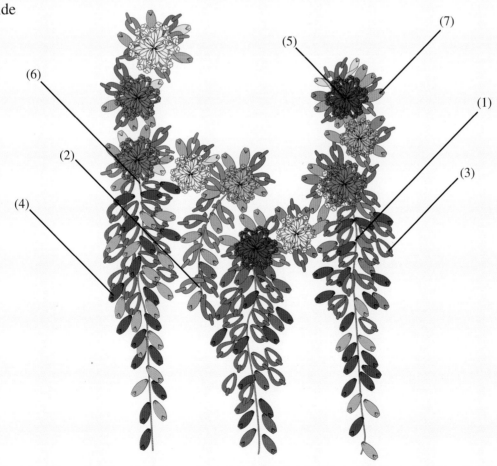

Quilted Bible Cover

Model size is 9¼" x 12"

Materials

- Beads: indigo seed (1 pkg.); 4mm round pink (4)
- Chenille: 1⅛"-wide bronze (½ yd.)
- Fabric: muslin — 12" x 15"; velvet — 44-60"-wide brown (½ yd.); 9-12 assorted fabric scraps in 4" x 6" pieces or odd shapes
- Lace: 3"-wide brown vintage in two different styles in 5-9" pieces
- Lightweight cardboard: 37" x 12"
- Quilt batting: 9¼" x 12½"
- Ribbon: silk — 4mm orange-gold (½ yd.); sea green (2 yds.); dk. rose (2 yds.); taupe (1¼ yds.); 7mm lt. burgundy (1¼ yds.); variegated dk. green (2 yds.); dk. red (1¼ yds.); velvet — ⅜"-wide burgundy (½ yd.)
- Silk floss: ecru, gold, lt. gold, blush pink, dusty purple, bright rose (1 pkg. each)
- Trim: ⅝"-wide gold/blue metallic (1¼ yds.); ⅞"-wide vintage beaded fringe (⅔ yd.)

Additional General Supplies & Tools
- General Supplies & Tools on page 109
- Needles: beading; size 20 chenille

Instructions

Refer to General Instructions on pages 8-16 for Bible Cover Assembling and for ribbon work and stitches that are used for this project.

1. Cut cardboard.

2. Cut velvet fabric for inner pocket front, inner pocket back, back, and spine.

3. Cut muslin fabric 1" larger all around for front.

4. Trim two fabric scrap pieces so one edge of each piece is the same length. Stitch onto muslin front, right sides together, taking ¼" seam along same-size edge. Open out and press. Vary fabric scraps and continue to stitch different sized pieces onto each other, right sides together. Trim outer edges to fit desired shape or area after piecing is finished. Overlap two fabric scraps with lace. Fill entire muslin front with fabric scraps. Open out pieces and press after each seam. Embroider desired stitches along seams of quilt pieces using silk flosses.

5. Embroider quilted front following Stitch Guide on page 116. Hand-stitch beaded fringe trim to quilted front as desired. Cut four 3" circles from fabric scraps to make yo-yos. Allow ¼" seam allowance. Stitch gathering stitch ¼" along circumference of each circle. Draw up circles and tuck raw edges into center of yo-yos. Press flat with the gathering. Tack to crazy-quilted front as desired. Tack seed beads around outer edges of yo-yos and round pink beads in center of yo-yos. Stitch leaves around yo-yos as desired using variegated dk. green silk ribbon and a Lazy Daisy Stitch.

6. Assemble spine.

7. Assemble bible cover. With wrong sides together, glue back to inner pocket. Glue edge of metallic trim to underside edge of front. With wrong sides together, glue front to inner pocket front. Glue one end of velvet ribbon to inside spine of bible. Drape ribbon through bible page. Knot ribbon end.

Stitch Guide

Description	Ribbon	Stitch
1. Mums, bottom layer	7mm dk. red	Knotted and Looped Ribbon Stitch
2. Mums, top layer	7mm lt. burgundy	Knotted and Looped Ribbon Stitch
3. Mum stamens	4mm taupe	Ribbon Stitch, 1-twist
4. Mum stamens	4mm orange-gold	Ribbon Stitch, 1-twist
5. Mum leaves, stems	7mm variegated dk. green chenille	Lazy Daisy Stitch, Twisted Ribbon, Couched Twisted Ribbon Stitch tacked with seed beads
6. Vines		
7. Buds along vine	4mm dk. rose	Lazy Daisy Stitch
8. Leaves along vine	4mm sea green	Ribbon Stitch, 1-twist

Stitch Guide

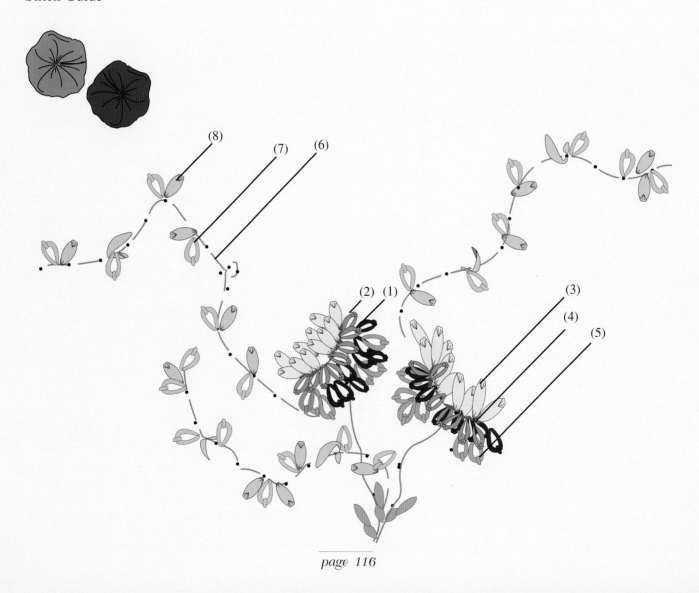

$\mathcal{M}$emory Album

Photo on page 117.

Materials
- Beads: bugle — size 2 cream, crystal, gold (1 pkg. each) ; size 5 mauve (1 pkg. each); seed — champagne, champagne ice, cream (1 pkg. each); round — 3mm old pearl (13)
- Bridal illusion: 15" square ivory
- Cording: 1/16"-wide gold (1½ yds.)
- Cross: 1" x ½" crystal
- Embroidery floss: gold
- Fabric: velveteen — 44"-wide ivory (½ yd.); moiré — 44-54"-wide ivory (14" square); muslin — 44"-wide natural (15" square); assorted — 7" squares of ivory-colored scraps (8-10)
- Lace: assorted sizes of ivory-colored scraps (8-10)
- Lightweight cardboard: 12" x 24" white
- Post-bound album: 12" square white
- Ribbon: brocade — 25mm ivory (½ yd.); metallic — 8mm bright gold (½ yd.); 15mm burnished gold (½ yd.); sheer — ½"-wide ivory with gold edge (2½ yds.); 15mm lt. brown with gold edge (½ yd.); silk — 4mm pale blue, ecru, ivory (2 yds. each); wire-edge — ⅝"-wide gold (½ yd.)

General Supplies & Tools
- Coordinating thread
- Craft glue: thin-bodied
- Needles: beading; size 3 embroidery; hand-sewing
- Paint roller with tray: 3" disposable
- Paintbrush
- Pins
- Rags: wet; dry
- Scissors: craft; fabric
- Screwdriver
- Sewing machine

Instructions
Refer to General Instructions on pages 12-16 for ribbon work and stitches that are used for this project.

1. Measure front of album cover. Subtract ⅛" from width and height measurements. Cut two pieces from lightweight cardboard according to measurements using craft scissors. Label width and height.

2. Unscrew posts that hold album together, using a screwdriver. Remove pages from album and set aside. Album is now in two pieces.

3. Measure album with inner flap opened out. Add 1" all around to width and height measurements. Cut two pieces from velveteen fabric according to measurements using fabric scissors. Label one piece as inside front and one as inside back. Label moire fabric as back cover.

4. Randomly machine- or hand-stitch assorted fabric scraps to muslin fabric for textured front. This technique is entirely free form. There are no rules to follow, except that when completed, all elements should flow together. It is not necessary for the pieces to be square — any shape will do. Apply some scraps so they are flat against muslin fabric. For other scraps, stitch only one edge in place. This will make it possible to later texture the fabric. Pin fabric scraps with the free edges to muslin fabric in a puckered, pleated, or randomly folded manner. Hand-tack puckers, etc. in place onto muslin fabric. Press flat from wrong side. Cover the flat fabric scraps with random pieces, sizes, and types of lace scraps. Some of the lace pieces can be puckered, etc., in same manner as with fabric scraps. It is not necessary to completely cover a fabric scrap with a lace.

5. Drape and pin sheer ivory ribbon over textured front by folding ribbon back and forth.

Criss-cross ribbon over textured front in many locations to achieve a gossamer feel. When pleased with arrangement, invisibly hand-tack ribbon in place over textured front.

6. Refer to Stitch Guide on page 120 for placement and ribbon color for Star of Bethlehem. To make a Star of Bethlehem, make six Star Petals. Individually hand-tack in place to textured front top right side. Make six Folded Leaves. Press leaves flat with iron. Do not join. Hand-tack in place in-between gold star petals. Make six Daisy Petals. Chain gather-stitch together. Position petals over gold wire-edge layer and tack in place. Make six Dahlias, Single Fold. Chain gather-stitch together. Position petals over lt. brown sheer layer and tack in place. Make six Folded Leaves. Chain gather-stitch together. Center and tack over brocade layer. Make twelve star rays.

7. Embellish star using mauve and cream bugle beads, and cream and champagne ice seed beads. Place as desired.

8. Randomly embroider small stars using ecru, ivory, and pale blue silk ribbon and the Cross-over Lazy Daisy Stitch. Stitch gold or cream bugle beads in-between petals. Stitch champagne seed beads at tips of ecru and ivory stars. Stitch an old pearl bead in center of each ecru and ivory star.

9. Overlay bridal illusion onto textured front. Stitch to muslin fabric at edges. Bead center of Star of Bethlehem with cream seed bead tipped with mauve bugle beads. Stitch crystal cross over top center of star. Anchor in place with champagne ice seed beads. Stitch crystal bugle beads near cross. Stitch crystal bugle beads in-between pale blue star petals. Stitch cream seed beads at tips of pale blue stars. Stitch an old pearl bead in the center of each pale blue star.

10. Drape and pin sheer ivory ribbon over bridal illusion in two locations in same manner as before. Hand-tack in place with cream seed beads.

11. Refer to General Instructions for Laminating on page 10. Laminate inside front and inside back of album with velveteen fabric. Trim bulk, leaving about ⅛" excess fabric at corners. Wrap fabric around to right side of album. When fabric has dried ten minutes, fold scrapbook on original scores and puncture post holes with tip of scissors. Laminate moire fabric to cardboard back. Trim bulk from corners and finish all four edges.

12. Laminate textured front to cardboard front in the same manner as for back.

13. Use roller to cover underside of moiré back with a thin layer of glue. Position wrong side of back centered onto right side of album back. Work with cardboard piece so that it thoroughly adheres at all outer edges to album back. This will take about five minutes. Set it aside for five minutes, then repeat adhering process. Repeat process with textured front and album front.

14. Use paint brush to place a thin bead of glue around outer edges of cardboard front only. Place cording over glued edge. Work with cording until it has adhered to front edge. Invisibly begin and end cording at bottom left corner.

15. Replace pages and posts into album and screw in place.

Stitch Guide

Description	Ribbon	Technique
1. Bottom layer	gold wire-edge	Star Petal
2. Bottom layer	lt. brown sheer	Folded Leaf
3. Middle layer	bright gold metallic	Daisy Petal
4. Middle layer	ivory brocade	Single Fold Dahlia
5. Top layer	burnished gold metallic	Folded Leaf
6. Star rays	gold floss	Long Straight Stitch

Stitch Guide

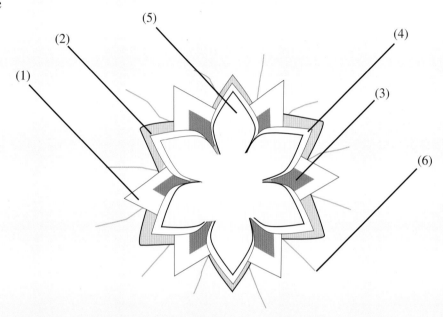

Christmas Album

Materials
- Braid: ¹⁄₁₆"-wide metallic gold (1⅛ yds.)
- Brass charms: 1" bee; 1" corner brackets (4)
- Cording: ⅛"-wide metallic gold (1½ yds.); ¹⁄₁₆"-wide green rattail; ⅛"-wide olive green
- Double-sided adhesive tape
- Embroidery floss: metallic gold, green, lt. green
- Fabric: embroidery — 12" x 17"; velvet — burgundy (1 yd.)
- Lightweight cardboard: 10½" x 15½"
- Photo album brackets (2)
- Ribbon: satin — ¼"-wide green, ½"-wide purple iridescent; silk — 4mm bronze, green, dk. green, lt. green, orange, red, lt. red, dk. red, rose, lt. rose, dk. rose; 7mm green, lt. green; velvet — ³⁄₁₆"-wide burgundy, green, red; wire-edge — ⅝"-wide green/peach ombré
- Stratacore: 18" x 28"
- Trim: ⅛"-wide burgundy picot

General Supplies & Tools
- Craft glue
- Craft knife
- Erasable marking pen
- Découpage medium

Continued on page 122.

Continued from page 120.
- Fabric scissors
- Needles: embroidery; hand-sewing
- Thread: coordinating; metallic gold; invisible

Instructions
Refer to General Instructions on pages 12-16 for ribbon work and stitches that are used for this project.

1. Use Christmas Album Placement Diagram on page 123 as general pattern for positioning ribbon onto embroidery fabric, using erasable marking pen. Place braid on fabric, forming the letter "C". Couch strands with invisible thread to secure.

2. Place green velvet ribbon in a diamond shape at center of fabric; tack with invisible thread to secure. Zigzag-stitch over velvet ribbon using two strands of gold metallic thread.

3. Place burgundy velvet ribbon to outer edge of design to frame; tack using invisible thread to secure. Place burgundy picot trim to inner borders of design; tack with invisible thread to secure.

4. Stitch two Ribbon Stitches and three Cross-over Lazy Daisy Stitches using orange 4mm silk ribbon.

5. Stitch Looped Ribbon Stitch to form center of flower using green 4mm silk ribbon.

6. Stitch one Bullion Lazy Daisy Stitch to form leaf using bronze 4mm silk ribbon.

7. For carnation, place thin green rattail on fabric to form stems. Couch with green floss to secure. Stitch short ends of a 12" length of ½"-wide purple iridescent satin ribbon together to form a tube. Stitch a gathering stitch on one edge of tube. Pull tightly to gather into a circular ruffle and secure thread. Repeat process to make three carnations. Stitch each flower to stem so that the flower lays open. Tack edges to create different effects as desired.

8. Stitch a large Ribbon Stitch for calyx using green ¼"-wide satin ribbon.

9. Stitch one long Ribbon Stitch, 1-Twist to form leaves using two shades of green 4mm silk ribbon.

10. For chrysanthemum, place green cording on fabric to form stems. Couch with lt. green floss to secure. Cut fifteen 3" lengths of three shades of rose 4mm silk ribbon. (For smaller mum, use ten 3" lengths.) Tie knot in center of each length. Refer to Diagram 1. Fold knotted length in half. Place lengths side by side and stitch a gathering stitch with a ⅝" seam. Pull tightly to gather. Join the first and last lengths. Trim seam to ⅛". Hand-sew to stem.

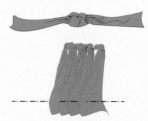

Diagram 1

11. For spider mum, alternately use three shades of red 4mm silk ribbon. Stitch center of spider mum with a Bullion Lazy Daisy Stitch. Refer to Diagram 2. Stitch three Twisted Ribbon Stitches. Continue to fill area with Twisted Ribbon Stitches. Stitch Looped Ribbon Stitches in a cluster with the darkest shade of ribbon. Stitch a combination of leaves using the Bullion Lazy Daisy Stitch and the Ribbon Stitch in two shades of green 4mm silk ribbon.

Diagram 2

12. For coleus leaves, cut a 5" length of ⅝"-wide wire-edge ribbon. Refer to Diagram 3. Fold ribbon in half, matching short ends. Turn folded ribbon corners up ⅛" from top edge. Following dashed line, stitch with gathering stitches. Pull thread so ribbon measures 1½" long. Secure thread. Open and shape leaf. Tack leaf to fabric, hiding raw edge.

Diagram 3

13. For cockscomb, tie red and burgundy shades of ³⁄₁₆"-wide velvet ribbon into twelve knots each. Trim each knot so ⅛" of ribbon remains on each side of knot. Stitch knots bunched together on fabric, alternating colors and hiding raw edges under other knots. Stitch Ribbon Stitches next to knotted ribbon bunches for leaves using two shades of green 7mm silk ribbon.

14. Glue quilt batting to cardboard, then center embroidered fabric on cardboard. Wrap excess fabric to back of cardboard and glue to secure. Glue brass corner brackets at points on green

velvet diamond. Glue bee charm to embroidered fabric as desired.

15. Mark and score a 1¾"-wide spine down center of stratacore to form an album cover. Cut burgundy velvet fabric into two 19" x 29" rectangles. Get velvet wet. Crumple to expel excess water. Loosely unfold. Allow to dry. Lay cover, scored side down, onto wrong side of one velvet fabric piece. Apply double-sided adhesive tape around edges of fabric and wrap to inside of cover. Apply a thin strip of adhesive tape to wrong side

edge of second fabric piece. Fold in ½". Apply découpage medium along folded edge of fabric. Place fabric wrong side down on inside of cover and press along edges to secure.

16. Mark placement for photo album brackets along spine. Poke a hole through spine and attach brackets.

17. Center and glue embroidered fabric to front of cover. Refer to photo on page 121 and glue metallic gold cording around edge of embroidered fabric.

Christmas Album Placement Diagram

Miss Katie McCall
25 Christmas Avenue

Seek where bygone summer
Have dropped their roses fair
A little Christmas package
Is waiting for you there.

"The orange-scented zephyrs
stirred, the branches rustled,
and the tinsel crackled like
merry-music, to which the
sparkling lights danced."
— E.T.A. Hoffman, "The Nutcracker"

Cards & Envelopes

Photo on page 124.

Materials

- Handmade papers: 5" x 16" for each envelope; 10" x 2¼" for each card
- Motifs: 1" square fabric or greeting card for each envelope
- Stickers: as desired for each envelope
- Watercolors: green, red

General Supplies & Tools

- Craft glue
- Marker: coordinating fine tip felt or colored pencil
- Paintbrush: small
- Scissors: craft; decorative paper edgers; pinking shears

Instructions

1. Trace enlarged Envelope Pattern below onto desired handmade paper and cut out. Fold side flaps inward along dotted lines. Fold bottom section inward along dotted line and glue to side flaps. Allow to dry. Fold top section inward along dotted line to form envelope flap.

2. Fold card paper in half and write desired poem or messages on front using a felt tip marker or colored pencil. Trim edges of card using decorative paper edgers.

3. Cut edges of motif using pinking shears to form a stamp. Tear a small piece of handmade paper to lay behind stamp. Paint paper with watercolors and allow to dry, then glue paper to top right corner of envelope. Glue stamp motif on top of paper.

4. Address front of envelope using a marker or colored pencil. Seal envelope flap with a sticker.

Envelope Pattern   Enlarge 260%

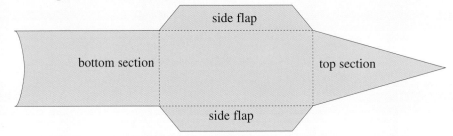

side flap

bottom section

top section

side flap

Memory Pillow

Photo on page 125.

Materials

- Coordinating thread
- Decorative pillow: as desired
- Wire-edge ribbon: 2"-wide (three times area of finished pillow)

General Tools & Supplies

- Hand-sewing needles

Instructions

1. Fold ribbon in half length wise. Pull wire in ribbon to gather. Tuck opposite ends under to secure.

2. Whip-stitch folded ribbon to pillow edge.

3. Match right sides of ribbon ends together and whip-stitch together. Tack to secure.

Note: A purchased hand-painted pillow can be embellished with a ribbon edge or an unique pillow can be created by placing a color copy of desired photo or artwork on desired pillow. Use photo transfer medium to transfer color copy to pillow. The transfer can then be embellished with fabric paint.

Metric Equivalency Chart

mm-millimetres cm-centimetres
inches to millimetres and centimetres

inches	mm	cm	inches	cm	inches	cm
⅛	3	0.3	9	22.9	30	76.2
¼	6	0.6	10	25.4	31	78.7
½	13	1.3	12	30.5	33	83.8
⅝	16	1.6	13	33.0	34	86.4
¾	19	1.9	14	35.6	35	88.9
⅞	22	2.2	15	38.1	36	91.4
1	25	2.5	16	40.6	37	94.0
1¼	32	3.2	17	43.2	38	96.5
1½	38	3.8	18	45.7	39	99.1
1¾	44	4.4	19	48.3	40	101.6
2	51	5.1	20	50.8	41	104.1
2½	64	6.4	21	53.3	42	106.7
3	76	7.6	22	55.9	43	109.2
3½	89	8.9	23	58.4	44	111.8
4	102	10.2	24	61.0	45	114.3
4½	114	11.4	25	63.5	46	116.8
5	127	12.7	26	66.0	47	119.4
6	152	15.2	27	68.6	48	121.9
7	178	17.8	28	71.1	49	124.5
8	203	20.3	29	73.7	50	127.0

yards to metres

yards	metres	yards	metres	yards	metres	yards	metres	yards	metres
⅛	0.11	2⅛	1.94	4⅛	3.77	6⅛	5.60	8⅛	7.43
¼	0.23	2¼	2.06	4¼	3.89	6¼	5.72	8¼	7.54
⅜	0.34	2⅜	2.17	4⅜	4.00	6⅜	5.83	8⅜	7.66
½	0.46	2½	2.29	4½	4.11	6½	5.94	8½	7.77
⅝	0.57	2⅝	2.40	4⅝	4.23	6⅝	6.06	8⅝	7.89
¾	0.69	2¾	2.51	4¾	4.34	6¾	6.17	8¾	8.00
⅞	0.80	2⅞	2.63	4⅞	4.46	6⅞	6.29	8⅞	8.12
1	0.91	3	2.74	5	4.57	7	6.40	9	8.23
1⅛	1.03	3⅛	2.86	5⅛	4.69	7⅛	6.52	9⅛	8.34
1¼	1.14	3¼	2.97	5¼	4.80	7¼	6.63	9¼	8.46
1⅜	1.26	3⅜	3.09	5⅜	4.91	7⅜	6.74	9⅜	8.57
1½	1.37	3½	3.20	5½	5.03	7½	6.86	9½	8.69
1⅝	1.49	3⅝	3.31	5⅝	5.14	7⅝	6.97	9⅝	8.80
1¾	1.60	3¾	3.43	5¾	5.26	7¾	7.09	9¾	8.92
1⅞	1.71	3⅞	3.54	5⅞	5.37	7⅞	7.20	9⅞	9.03
2	1.83	4	3.66	6	5.49	8	7.32	10	9.14

Index